Women and Religion

Women and Religion

—⁂—

Majella Franzmann

New York   Oxford
OXFORD UNIVERSITY PRESS
2000

Oxford University Press

Oxford   New York
Athens   Auckland   Bangkok   Bogotá   Buenos Aires   Calcutta
Cape Town   Chennai   Dar es Salaam   Delhi   Florence   Hong Kong
Istanbul
Karachi   Kuala Lumpur   Madrid   Melbourne   Mexico City   Mumbai
Nairobi   Paris   São Paulo   Singapore   Taipei   Tokyo   Toronto
Warsaw

and associated companies in
Berlin   Ibadan

Published by Oxford University Press, Inc.,
198 Madison Avenue, New York, New York, 10016
http://www.oup-usa.org
1-800-334-4249

Library of Congress Cataloging-in-Publication Data
Franzmann, Majella, 1952–
Women and religion / by Majella Franzmann.
p.   cm.
Includes bibliographical references and index.
ISBN 0-19-510773-X (pbk. : alk. paper)
1. Women and religion.   I. Title.
BL458.F67   1999
200'.82—dc21   99-26247
CIP

Printing (last digit): 9 8 7 6 5 4 3 2 1

Printed in the United States of America
on acid-free paper

This book is dedicated to
Mary Patricia Franzmann,
November 1, 1909–November 1, 1992

Contents

—m—

Preface

—⚮—

Teaching a university course entitled "Women and Religion" is a rare experience within academic life. Although I have become accustomed to the fine interplay of personal and academic concerns when dealing with all the units offered in the Studies in Religion program, no other unit calls forth quite the same mix of intensity of discussion and involvement of students, of emotional reaction to the material for study, or of self-disclosure, both from students and from me as teacher.

My classes on women and religion generally comprise Studies in Religion students, students with a background in women's studies or feminist philosophy, and others who are simply taking the class out of personal interest. As would be expected, the social backgrounds and ages of the students are extremely disparate, as are their relationships to any form of religion or spirituality. Some students have had little or no contact with religious tradition; some are committed to a tradition; others have left a tradition in which they were once involved; still others struggle to stay committed to a tradition. And there are those who are searching out new forms of religious expression, some having fun in the search, and some for whom the search has become a matter of real struggle and survival.

Although students are from a variety of backgrounds, both personal and academic, their reactions in my classes to the material we study are often similar—various levels of distress at the negative treatment of women in religious traditions, some positive reactions to attempts to reinterpret and reevaluate women's business within the traditions, but mostly either outright condemnation of religions for the varieties of abuse visited upon women or an unease stemming from wanting to make such condemnations but not feeling justified in making judgments against groups from other cultures or times. This unease is often brought out forcibly in reaction to the extreme cases in which women apparently choose freely to participate in what are seen to be limiting situations.

Let me say at the outset that regardless of the philosophical or moral implications of any discussion about women's religious experience, women and men will still read and listen to stories about such experience. In this book, I attempt at least to provide a process by which reading and listening can be done with integrity. Because I cannot hope to cover the enormous amount of material available within the area of women and religion, but only draw out some of the major themes and issues, the model can serve the reader in further work.

This study was first proposed and begun by two authors but has ended up as a solo work. I wish to thank most especially Ursula Janey O'Shea for the hard work and lively discussion in the early stages of the planning and writing. I am grateful to Joan Relke for most of the initial detailed research work; to Jeff Hodges for editing, proofreading, and making suggestions on each draft of the manuscript; and to Toni Tidswell for help in the final stages of preparing the manuscript. Thanks also to those who gave their time generously to read various sections and draft chapters: Toni Tidswell, Elaine Wainwright, and Kathryn Hedemann. I wish also to pay tribute to my many students over the five years I have been at the University of New England—especially those who took my classes in Women and Religion—who have helped me to clarify my thinking on so many of the issues in this book, but especially in the area of hermeneutics.

Finally, I would like to thank most sincerely Cynthia Read, senior editor at Oxford University Press, who supported the project so positively in the early stages, and her successor Robert Miller, who encouraged the work to final publication.

I dedicate this work to my mother, who might not have agreed with much that I have written in this book, but whose life is inextricably bound to mine.

Introduction

In setting out to study any subject, the student is often presented a simple model comprising three major elements—(1) a person using (2) a method to study (3) something; that is, the student is the subject, the something being studied is the object, and the link between the two is the method of study. In this book I want to take a very different tack. Especially for study within the humanities and social sciences, the sharp distinction between subject and object is not only unhelpful but unrealistic. Trying to dissolve the distinction allows a number of important processes to come into focus: It allows the material being studied to speak rather than to be scrutinized; it allows the one who studies to see more clearly that even the first engagement with the material is an exercise in finding a point of contact, a link, a common meeting ground; and it gives a more realistic view of study as an integrating process of listening both to someone/something else and to oneself (self-reflection). In other words, the process of study should cause students to engage *themselves* in conversation as much as to engage with the material they wish to study, and then

1

to take the conversation further in ever-widening circles into their own lived experience.

In this book, then, I want to suggest that instead of women and their religious experience being seen as the objects of study, women be allowed to be the subjects. Now, of course, there is a difficulty if the reader wants to understand this in a very literal sense. Lengthy quotations or major excerpts from women's writings are not appropriate in a book of this kind, being more suited to anthologies, or to books that present material in case studies, or to books by individual women about their own spiritual questing. Some examples of such works are listed in the suggested readings at the end of this book.

What I want to propose, rather, is a kind of second-level shift in the reader, to an attitude of listening in a different way to the experience of women, letting the women be speaking subjects. Of course, there will be difficulties in wanting to hear women say "I/we," "me/our" in the sources rather than having religious traditions say "they/them" about women. The reader will be confronted with examples of women's religious experience described by scholars or by male religious professionals; or by examples of texts and practices within traditions where women do not figure, do not speak, or are to be found only on the edge of descriptions about the dominant religious or social group.

How is the reader to allow the women to be subjects? Some simple techniques can be helpful. Imagine that you can change the pronouns "they/them" used by the scholars and clerics to "we/us" by the women subjects, and how the women might tell a different story of their experience. Where a woman appears in a story only as a secondary figure or as one who does not speak, imagine that she moves to center stage, and see the story unfold again from her point of view. Where women's religious practice is relegated by the dominant group to the domestic sphere, place the woman and her domestic setting in the center of the social and religious network and imagine how she might speak of the value of her religious practice in this space that is hers above all. I deal with some of these techniques in a little more detail in chapter 4.

The last suggestion raises a very important point that will become clearer later in the book: Women frequently lead religious lives that are quite separate from the normative sphere of religious activity described by the major established religions. While I have suggested in the last paragraph ways in which the student might attempt to revalue women's experience and redress the marginalization of women within male-dominated public rituals and texts, doing this must be balanced by trying to understand how the alternative religious lives of women have operated outside of this normative sphere. Once women are allowed to speak about their own space, rather than have male religious professionals speak for them from the male-dominated space, an entirely other world of experience may be identified.

As well as listening to the voices of women, we need to ask ourselves *how* we are listening to these voices. How ready are we, for example, to respond to voices that may cause us some distress or unease or shock? We have to be careful, too, that we have not already decided, even before we begin to listen, what we expect or would like to hear.

In suggesting that we concentrate on listening to women's experiences, I do not want to suggest necessarily that these experiences have a privileged place or an extra level of authority within any religious tradition. On the other hand, I do not agree that these stories of experience are in any way secondary in importance to what might be traditionally presented as key aspects of a particular tradition. This point is made occasionally in the backlash to some feminist theologians who use women's experience as a kind of higher authority in criticism of religious traditions and their practices.[1]

If you have looked at other books devoted to the topic of women and religion, you will notice immediately that what I am trying to do is different from the norm. Usually, such books divide the information and discussion into specific religious traditions ("Women in Judaism," "Women in Hinduism," etc.) or specific cultures ("Chinese religions," etc.). In this book, I try to draw together major themes and issues for women and religion across traditions and cultures.[2] In writing in this way, I am obviously im-

plicitly proposing that there is some connection between the varieties of women's experiences regardless of cultural and temporal differences. Is there a link simply by virtue of the fact that all
of the speakers are women? Or is there something essentially different about any woman's experience compared with any man's
experience?

Before I begin with the detailed outline of how to read—or
how to listen—in the following chapters, I need to ask questions
that are very basic, like "What is a woman?," "What is experience?,"
"What is a woman's experience?"

WHAT IS A WOMAN?

There are those who presently argue vehemently that there is
something essential, some essence, in women that makes them
different from men, whether that essence is a connection with nature or a maternal instinct or something else. Most of these pre-
sentations seem to be based on a view of a woman's biological
make-up, or perhaps I should say the biological make-up of the
majority of those who identify themselves as women.

On the other hand, there are those who are just as strongly
convinced that there is no essence:

> One woman + one woman + one woman will never add up to
> some generic entity: woman.[3]

Some scholars see the latter position as undermining what
progress has been made by women's movements. Kate Soper
speaks of a move to an "extreme particularism," "a hyper-indi-
vidualism," and argues that "feminism as theory has pulled the
rug from under feminism as politics"; that is, it has taken away
that focus on solidarity and a common voice for the previously
isolated and silent women that so characterized the earliest feminist movements.[4]

I do not hold the position that there is something essentially
different about women, but I do not think this fact should stop

me from speaking about women as a group and about their experiences.

WHAT IS A WOMAN'S EXPERIENCE?

Some scholars writing on women's religious experience use the
term *experience* without explaining what they mean by it. Others
offer some brief definition. Ursula King, for example, writes, "Experience as simply lived and happening is the raw material and
matrix for reflection,"[5] which has echoes of earlier work by
philosophers like Dilthey, who suggests that experience is something we live in and through and which can only subsequently become the object of reflection, and Gadamer, who writes that the
knowing that happens in experience is not conceptual but a happening, an event, an encounter.[6]

King is careful to distinguish between the terms *feminine, female,*
and *feminist* when speaking of experience. Over the twentieth century, feminists have been particularly anxious to critique the
traditional roles and images of what was called "female" and "feminine," a process that has been aided by the increasing international dimension and pluralism of women's experience as well as
women's new social and work experiences.[7]

As King states, much of the new feminist interpretation has focused on female bodily experience as a means of understanding
women's experience. This is not unproblematical, since the ide-
alization of women's experience in terms of the uniqueness of female bodily experience acts against the feminist critique of the
concept of "biology as destiny." King sums up, "Female bodily existence is a primary source of women's self-image and destiny, but
not an exclusive one."[8]

Judith Grant studies this area in some depth in relation to theories about knowledge, showing that some current feminist theories fall into the trap of assuming that rationality and objectivity are male modes of knowing and that female knowledge
proceeds from female bodily experience, especially that of mothering. As Grant argues, "It is not obvious, however, precisely what

it is about the female reproductive system that would make women think differently than men."[9] To suggest that rational ways of knowing are male and not female makes "the implicit assertion that the sex of one's body is at least as significant as the condition of one's mind in assessing one's reason."[10]

Since the earlier critique of the traditional stereotypical use of "female" and "feminine" and of the arguments that sexual difference is determined by nature/natural forces, there has been a shift to understandings of gender "as less a set of discrete indices of difference, and more as a category of human experience,"[11] and a belief that social relations determine sex differences rather than biological sex producing social division between the sexes.[12] Elaine Graham notes the current move from concerns with sex and gender to concerns with power and difference, a move from gender understood as an individualistic character trait to "analyses of the systemic and structural patterns of differentiation."[13] This pattern is repeated in debates about patriarchy, which I discuss below. Thus, more contemporary theories of gender have made the shift to broader analyses of social order and human behavior, many using multidisciplinary or interdisciplinary approaches (from anthropology, psychology, biological sciences, sociology and social theory, history, philosophy, and cultural studies).[14]

Serene Jones takes nine publications from a variety of feminist, womanist (Black), and *mujerista* (Hispanic) theologians, and proposes to look at the kinds of methodological assumptions of each based on its conception of women's experience.[15] She finds that some authors essentialize the concept of experience in universalizing and/or ahistorical frames of reference; that is, they see women's experience within a more general account of the basic structure of human experience, even though they do not essentialize the concepts "woman" and "gender." The others localize the concept of experience in history and within specific cultural frames of reference. Although drawn to the second group on methodological grounds, Jones finds that she favors the substance of the work of the first group—the first group has "endurance" and the second "restlessness." She suggests that the challenge for the first group is those experiences that do not fit universalizing categories; for the second group it is the demand for a vision or for a faith-filled truth with substance—fragmentary selves are no good for those already oppressively fragmented.[16]

Taking a slightly different tack, Judith Grant looks at feminist theories about female knowledge based on female experience, suggesting that feminists use two different ways of looking at the issue: either as "woman's experience," by which they tend to impute some kind of universal female experience (often "mothering"),[17] or as "women's experiences," by which it is suggested that the experiences of various types or groups of women are different "perspectives" of the larger "Female Experience." In other words, for the latter the experience of Woman is the sum of the specific experiences of different women.[18] As Grant points out, problems arise with this idea when two experiences or perspectives of women come into conflict. Grant uses the example of recent debates in which those who advocate lesbian sadomasochistic activity (and are hence seen to be involved in forms of behavior based on dominant/submissive roles) have come into conflict with women who hold that any form of sex involving domination is pornography.[19] Grant concludes by stating her opposition to a theory about female knowledge based on experience: First, such theories always seem to lead the theorist back to biological women; and second, she is unconvinced that the boundaries between male and female, intuition and rationality, are as clear as feminist theorists have thus far assumed.[20]

PATRIARCHY

Associated with the attempt at redefining the terms *female, feminine,* and so on, patriarchy and its trademark of gender oppression were the first targets of the feminist movement. The term *patriarchy* literally means "rule of the fathers" (from two Greek words πατήρ [patēr] = father, and ἄρχω [archō] = rule). Ursula King defines patriarchy as "a male power and property structure in which men are dominant to the detriment of women and, one

may add, also largely to the detriment of their own full development."[21] However, she goes on to speak of the social, economic, religious, and political power structures of patriarchy
and also of its deep rootedness in attitudes, values, language,
and thought.[22] King also cites Kate Millett's proposal that perhaps patriarchy is even more a habit of mind and a way of life
than a political system.[23] Dolores Williams also characterizes patriarchy in terms of gender oppression, even when including oppression by institutions: as "the power relation between men and
women and between women and society's institutions controlled
by men."[24]

Some feminists have gradually been defining patriarchy in such
a way that the term covers much broader issues than gender oppression. Letty Russell, for example, writes that, "The patriarchal
paradigm of reality places everything in a hierarchy of domination and subordination, accepting the marginalization of the pow-
erless as a given."[25] However, the problem remains that the term
itself, in its literal sense, is firmly tied to the idea of men oppressing women.

Sometimes the word "androcentrism" is also used in conjunction with the term patriarchy.[26] This word simply means that men
are in the center, that is, that the experience of men is taken as
the norm and of the most importance. If I were to suggest that
women's experience should be in the center, I would use the term
gynocentric, and if I were to suggest that experience of human beings should be in the center, I would use the term *anthropocentric*,
although this word is somewhat problematical since it presumes
to include people in general but is similar to the use of the word
"men" to include all human beings.

One of the early criticisms of the view that patriarchy and gender oppression were the central issues for all women came from
women of color, especially black women in the United States.
Black women asserted that white feminists had not been speaking for them, that the definition of patriarchy as women's chief
enemy was limited, since the oppression black women and other
women of color experienced was not only gender oppression but
a variety of oppressions from an interweaving of power relations

of race, class, and gender.[27] Thus Mary Hunt's suggestion that the only common element in women's experience is gender oppression is clearly wide of the mark with regard to black women's thinking.[28]

Black women assert that their experience has other dimensions than those white women experience. Much of their writing and their interpretation of texts and women's religious experience includes a consideration of the oppression experienced by black people in the past through slavery and segregation.[29] Especially disturbing is the history of abuse and complete exploitation of black women's bodies.[30]

As black feminist Audre Lorde pointed out in her open letter to white feminist Mary Daly, all women's experience of oppression is not the same. "The oppression of women knows no ethnic nor racial boundaries, true, but that does not mean it is identical within those boundaries."[31] In fact, Jacquelyn Grant asserts that white women's experience and black women's experience (especially of slavery and segregation) can really be said to be in "completely different realms."[32]

Dolores Williams sums up the problem of continuing to use the term patriarchy from the point of view of black feminists in this way:

> *Patriarchy*—as a term to describe black women's relation to the white (male and female) dominated social and economic systems governing their lives—leaves too much out. It is silent about class-privileged women oppressing women without class privilege. It is silent about white men and white women working together to maintain white supremacy and white privilege. It is silent about the positive boons patriarchy has bestowed upon many white women, for example, college education; the skills and credentials to walk into the jobs the civil rights movement obtained for women; in some cases the *choice* to stay home and raise children and/or develop a career—*and* to hire another woman (usually a black one) "to help out" in either case.[33]

For some black feminists, the feminist enterprise is seriously flawed then by two major issues—it is white and it is racist, that is, white feminists perpetuate white supremacy and do not include all women in their struggle for liberation.[34]

However, the conundrum of being involved in patriarchy by accepting its gifts of privilege even while working to be liberated from its oppression is not just a white problem. Williams herself speaks of the two-edged sword of black women's experience in the African-American denominational churches in North America where women are oppressed by sexism but where they also find sustenance and space for their religious life.[35] Williams admits too that she is among the educated elite within the black community and knows that she is privileged over poor uneducated women of all colors.[36] When speaking of the general oppression of women according to their inclusion in the patriarchal lower caste of "women," and the fact that some white women and black women may be able to speak together of common experiences within a similar socioeconomic class, Williams does not suggest why it might be that poor black women and privileged black women might be able to speak together better than poor black women and poor white women.[37]

In the end it seems to me that there may be another case here of essentializing experience, this time black and white experience. While Williams seems to speak for her black sisters, Diana Hayes, although black, appears to feel herself excluded from such black feminist theology because of her Catholic context.[38]

At stake in the discussion of how one might understand women's experience and the terms used by feminists to describe the conditions of that experience is the ability of women to work together despite their differences of experience, their priorities within the struggle for survival or for liberation, and their different philosophies. I return to this again to some extent in chapter 5. If such cooperation is to take place, then clearly the term *patriarchy* or some other term must express the totality of oppression experienced by women whatever their racial, cultural, class, religious, or economic circumstances. Early in the debate about the term patriarchy, womanist scholars seemed not to think that a revision would be possible. In her early work, for example, Williams used the term *demonarchy* as a sociopolitical and spiritual term for the particular experience of the black people especially with regard to slavery and white rule.[39] However, in *Sisters in the Wilderness*, Williams calls for just such a revision.[40]

What seems to be occurring now is a move to revise the terms thoroughly, rather than simply take the list of oppressions of which black, Hispanic, or Asian women speak and add them to the list of the sins of patriarchy. Scholars are now realizing that these are not parallel oppressions but rather multiplicative systems of oppression. Some, like Elisabeth Schüssler Fiorenza, are choosing to retain the more traditional terms *feminism* and *patriarchy*; while acknowledging the difficulties inherent in using them now, they show that they understand the breadth of the contemporary discussion.[41] Schüssler Fiorenza speaks of patriarchy as "a pyramid of interlocking dominations," but also has coined the term *kyriarchy* (adopted from the Greek κύριος [kyrios] ("lord," "master") for patriarchal power that operates on an institutional-structural level, with interlocking systems of oppression based on gender, race, class, culture, and religion.[42]

There is no doubting the difference in content and degree of oppression experienced in everyday circumstances by women. Although I understand the great differences, I think it might be possible to speak about a common structure in these various experiences. What I am seeking to do in this book is to find some patterns common to different experiences of women in order to present models for understanding individual experiences. Instead of the differences in the experience of oppression, I want to talk about the structure of the experiences themselves, since the structures of oppression and other experiences, even positive experiences for that matter, may be common.

While I presume to speak about other women's experiences and to try to find some common patterns in the structure of these experiences, I am also aware of some of the traps that can lie in wait for me. One of the concerns of those who oppose the attempt to represent other women's experience is that those white feminists who do so may be operating out of the mindset of colonialism in just as brutal a way as those who go to colonize people physically. In other words, I must be careful that in speaking of other women's experience, I am not trying to present them in my own image and likeness, not trying to tell them how they should be.

To return again to one of my first points, it seems essential in carrying out this study to listen attentively to the stories of women's experience if such problems are to be avoided. The intention to listen with attentiveness seems a first step in respecting the voices of the women speaking. The second step, and one that accompanies the listening at every stage of the process, is to listen to my own voice with attentiveness, to try to be aware even in a small way of the biases I hold that make a difference in the way I shape and make sense to myself of what these women are saying.

In this book, I suggest certain ways of interpreting women's religious experience. In suggesting a method, I give power to certain questions and patterning of information and results, even while urging you to take a critical stance toward all the material that you encounter. Needless to say, this book is another secondary source, and you need to be wary and critical of my methods. Being open to what I have to suggest as you read this book does not negate your responsibility to be critical.

I am an Australian woman of Irish and German descent who teaches in a small rural university in New South Wales. It would be naïve of me to think that every woman who reads this book would agree with my method of studying, or my various interpretations of, women's religious experience. There is no more guarantee of that happening within my own cultural context than across cultures, just as women even within the same religious traditions will not necessarily agree on issues or react to women's stories in the same way. While women have been marginalized in religious traditions when men have spoken for them, I—of course—risk doing the same thing to women in trying to give a taste of women's religious experience in general and in trying to show you how you might interpret or appreciate it.

I have attempted to write this book according to the hermeneutical principles that I set down in chapter 1. Naturally, I am not the only one who currently advocates placing women in the center as the subject of the study. Not all of those who advocate the process are successful at it. The problems may be very subtle. In speaking for other women, even with the best intentions, I may be not allowing them to speak for themselves, or I may even be silencing them once more in a repetition of what they have already experienced. Diane Purkiss criticizes Mary Daly's presentation of the figure of the witch in *Gyn/Ecology* for this reason, and it serves as a valuable warning to any researcher.[43]

I do not assume myself to be free of bias, but my methodology tries to make the bias in my own work, and in the sources that I use, transparent to you to test against your own experience.

Notes

1. See, e.g., Linda Woodhead, "Spiritualising the Sacred: A Critique of Feminist Theology," *Modern Theology*, vol. 13 (1997), pp. 191–92.

2. Perhaps the book that comes closest to doing this, but in a much briefer way, is Ursula King's *Women and Spirituality: Voices of Protest and Promise*, Women and Society (London: Macmillan Education, 1989), especially the section from pp. 38–58.

3. Luce Irigaray, *Speculum of the Other Woman*, tr. Gillian C. Gill. (Ithaca, N.Y.: Cornell University Press, 1985), p. 230. See also the study of Irigaray, Ruether, and Daly and their understanding of "woman" in relation to issues of race and class in Ellen T. Armour, "Questioning 'Woman' in Feminist/Womanist Theology: Irigaray, Ruether, and Daly," in C. W. Maggie Kim et al., eds., *Transfigurations: Theology and the French Feminists* (Minneapolis: Fortress Press, 1993), pp. 143–69.

4. Kate Soper, "Feminism, Humanism and Postmodernism," in Mary Evans, ed., *The Woman Question*, 2nd ed. (London: Sage Publications, 1994), pp. 14–15.

5. King, *Women and Spirituality*, p. 59. King's chapter 3, "Voices of Experience," is worth reading on this concept (pp. 59–90).

6. See the summaries of their theories in Richard E. Palmer, *Hermeneutics: Interpretation Theory in Schleiermacher, Dilthey, Heidegger, and Gadamer* (Evanston, Ill.: Northwestern University Press, 1969), pp. 108 and 195.

7. King, *Women and Spirituality*, pp. 60–72.

8. King, *Women and Spirituality*, p. 80.

9. Judith Grant, "I Feel Therefore I Am: A Critique of Female Experience as the Basis for a Feminist Epistemology," *Women and Politics*, vol. 7 (1987), p. 106. Mary E. Hawkesworth ("Feminist Epistemology: A Survey of the Field, *Women and Politics*, vol. 7 [1987]) covers the same area of discussion (pp. 120–22). See also Susan J. Hekman, *Gender and Knowledge: Elements of a Postmodern Feminism*, Northeastern Series in Feminist Theory (Boston: Northeastern University Press, 1990), pp. 135–51.

10. Judith Grant, "I Feel Therefore I Am," p. 105.

11. Elaine L. Graham, *Making the Difference: Gender, Personhood and Theology* (Minneapolis: Fortress Press, 1996), p. 11.

12. Graham, *Making the Difference*, p. 66. The entire chapter is useful reading: "Gender, Nature and Culture," pp. 64–70.

13. Graham, *Making the Difference*, pp. 22–24. Particularly helpful in this connection is Graham's further work in the section entitled "The Origins of Gender Hierarchy," pp. 70–76.

14. Graham, *Making the Difference*, pp. 24–25.

15. Serene Jones, "'Women's Experience' Between a Rock and a Hard Place: Feminist, Womanist and *Mujerista* Theologies in North America," *Religious Studies Review*, vol. 21 (1995), pp. 171–78.

16. Jones, "Women's Experience," p. 178.

17. Grant, "I Feel Therefore I Am," p. 108–9.

18. Grant, "I Feel Therefore I Am," p. 110.

19. Grant, "I Feel Therefore I Am," p. 110–11.

20. Grant, "I Feel Therefore I Am," p. 112–13.

21. King, *Women and Spirituality*, p. 22.

22. King, *Women and Spirituality*, p. 25.

23. Kate Millett, *Sexual Politics* (London: Rupert Hart-Davis, 1971), p. 63.

24. Dolores S. Williams, "The Color of Feminism: Or Speaking the Black Woman's Tongue," *The Journal of Religious Thought*, vol. 43 (1986), p. 47.

25. Letty M. Russell, *Church in the Round: Feminist Interpretation of the Church* (Louisville, Ky.: Westminster/John Knox Press, 1993), p. 35.

26. King (*Women and Spirituality*) defines androcentrism and gives a history of the term from Lester Ward (pp. 25–26).

27. Sometimes what appears to be gender oppression may be focused more on class than on gender. Thus Patricia Jeffery (*Frogs in a Well: Indian Women in Purdah*, London: Zed Press, 1979) shows that some of the

harsh practices women undergo in Hindu society (such as infanticide, *purdah* [seclusion from the public], and *sati* [voluntary suicide of women whose husbands have predeceased them]) have almost always been the practices of the most wealthy and privileged sectors of Hindu society rather than of the low-caste sector (p. 1).

28. Mary E. Hunt, "Friends in Deed," in Linda Hurcombe, ed., *Sex and God: Some Varieties of Women's Religious Experience* (New York: Routledge & Kegan Paul, 1987), p. 49.

29. See, e.g., Dolores S. Williams' (*Sisters in the Wilderness: The Challenge of Womanist God-Talk*, Maryknoll, N.Y.: Orbis Books, 1993) analysis of the Hagar story in the Book of Genesis in the Jewish scriptures (pp. 196–99).

30. Williams, *Sisters*, p. 202. Of all the material I have read in this connection, the most potent has been Alice Walker's "The Right to Life: What Can the White Man Say to the Black Woman?," in Charlotte Watson Sherman, ed., *Sisterfire: Black Womanist Fiction and Poetry* (New York: HarperPerennial, 1994), pp. 93–98.

31. Audre Lorde, "An Open Letter to Mary Daly," in Cherríe Moraga and Gloria Anzaldúa, eds., *This Bridge Called My Back: Writings by Radical Women of Color*, 2nd ed. (New York: Kitchen Table: Women of Color Press, 1983), p. 97. Lorde wrote the open letter to Daly out of her concern that Daly had used Lorde's writings in *Gyn/Ecology* to support a view of non-European women only as victims and those who prey upon each other (p. 94).

32. Jacquelyn Grant, *White Women's Christ and Black Women's Jesus: Feminist Christology and Womanist Response*, AAR Academy Series 64 (Atlanta, Ga.: Scholars Press, 1989), p. 195.

33. Williams, *Sisters*, p. 185.

34. See, e.g., the treatment of this issue in Williams, *Sisters*, p. 186, and Grant, *White Women's Christ*, pp. 195–230.

35. Williams, *Sisters*, p. xii–xiii.

36. Williams, *Sisters*, p. 186.

37. Williams, *Sisters*, p. 244, n. 7.

38. Diana L. Hayes, "Different Voices: Black, Womanist and Catholic," in Mary Phil Korsak, ed., *Voicing Identity: Women and Religious Traditions in Europe*, Conference Records, Fifth Biennial Conference at the University of Louvain, 16–20 August, 1993 (Louvain: European Society of Women in Theological Research), pp. 1–34.

39. Williams, "The Color of Feminism," pp. 52, 58.

40. Williams, *Sisters*, p. 186.

41. Elisabeth Schüssler Fiorenza, *But She Said: Feminist Practices of Biblical Interpretation* (Boston: Beacon Press, 1992), pp. 6–7, 115.

42. Schüssler Fiorenza, *But She Said*, p. 123.

43. Diane Purkiss (*The Witch in History: Early Modern and Twentieth-century Representations*, London: Routledge, 1996) suggests that Daly is uninterested in the things that the witches actually said or did, that Daly presents only the suffering bodies of the witches. Reducing a woman in this way to a "tortured, voiceless body," "goes beyond even the interrogators in removing subjectivity from a woman, who becomes nothing but an instructive spectacle of violation and dismemberment, offering no opportunity to the reader who wants to know her" (p. 14).

1

Hearing Voices—A Process for Reading and Writing About Women and Religion

—∞—

The process by which human beings understand, including the conditions under which that happens, is described generally by the term *hermeneutics*, from the Greek ἑρμηνεύω (hermēneuō), "to interpret, to explain, to make clear." The term was used by the Greeks to describe, among other things, the activity of translating from one language to another, and it is often used in Studies in Religion in the narrow sense to describe the process of understanding written texts. In this area of study, it has been used for the most part for the process of understanding or interpreting the Jewish and Christian scriptures.

For the purposes of this study, the term *hermeneutics* is used in a broad sense to cover the process and conditions of human understanding of anything that might be material for study: written or spoken words, rituals, authoritative statements, dance, song,

17

painting, drama, paraphernalia (dress, utensils, etc.), architecture, and so on. Attempting to understand something includes mental processes and psychological processes, but hermeneutics is also intensely interested in the place where a person stands— the place from which that person attempts to see the phenomenon to be understood—as well as the place where that phenomenon is situated.

When I speak of understanding, I do not imply that a person will necessarily know some kind of absolute truth about what is being studied. Sometimes, I may feel after studying a phenomenon that I am very far from understanding it, that I have more questions now than I had when I started on my quest to understand. So when I use the term *understanding*, I am really speaking more about a process of comprehending or apprehending, of being engaged with a phenomenon, rather than arriving at some definitive answer as to its meaning.

In outlining a possible process for understanding, I want first to emphasize the listening, analyzing, and judging capacity of the person studying in relation to the two key elements of the hermeneutic: the phenomenon and oneself.

For the phenomenon, you might ask questions like the following:

- What is the story of this phenomenon (what has happened to it through history, and how has it developed)?
- What does it tell me of the religious experience of those who cherish it or who are informed by it?
- Who has spoken of this text and attempted to really hear it and understand what it says (both believers and academics)?

At the same time, you might ask questions of yourself like the following:

- Where am I standing in order to listen to this material with my head and my heart?

- Am I listening as an outsider or as an insider, as one opposed or as one who is sympathetic?
- What kind of study has already "tuned" my ear to hear or has dulled my sense of hearing?
- In what way does this phenomenon move me personally?

In the introduction I spoke of the three elements of any study— the person studying, the method by which the person studies, and what is being studied, or, as I refer to it here, the phenomenon. I want you to try to imagine the process in which these elements are linked as very fluid. The person studying uses certain questions to begin to listen to the phenomenon, but even these questions will change as the phenomenon speaks. The student, too, will be constantly changing in position as he or she attempts to understand. The method used will change as the student changes position in relation to the phenomenon. Thus, the whole process is really like a very lively, open-ended dialogue in which the positions of the dialogue partners constantly change and new and interesting ideas come to light.

Perhaps you are surprised that the questions I have presented so far for both the phenomenon and the student include an emphasis on the emotional or psychological aspects that come under reflection in the hermeneutical process. Although the process of understanding is an academic exercise when one carries out studies in religion, this should not be taken to imply that it is a clear, objective, rational process, or that the understanding process should exclude a strong emotional or psychological aspect when a person studies by participating, for example, in Zen meditation or sacred dance. If I take seriously that the student is a human being, then I must consider all the levels of a human being that are at work in understanding, including all those levels of feeling and reaction that often guide a person's rational aspects in powerful and subtle ways. Thus, an integral part of the hermeneutical process involves reflecting on these levels at every stage of questioning, analysis, and making of critical judgments. In this way, my judgments about what I am trying to understand will never be just rational, academic judgments but will be integrated as completely as possible with all the other aspects, including the psychological, of my life in general.

This is a somewhat more involved hermeneutical process than you might find in general in academic circles, even though most scholars are aware of taking their emotional and psychological reactions into account when doing research. Yet, even though these reactions may be seen as positive elements of the process, many regard them as something added on or secondary to the more important intellectual process. What I want to suggest is a process within which the emotional and psychological elements are absolutely integral.

I am really advocating a process that includes what I would call critical discernment. *Discernment* is a term often used in a religious sense for a process by which an individual or community makes choices "methodically with God," to use the description of Pierre Wolff. As Wolff points out, discernment is not necessarily a religious activity; it is simply "a process that allows a person to see, without confusion and ambiguity, what differentiates things."[1] He sets out a simple schema of the major steps in such a process[2]: The framework is time; the tools are the head and the heart ("we screen with our heart in order to make a decision that is *ours* and one we can confirm subjectively"[3]); the cornerstone is values (I "weigh my options with respect to what is important to me"[4]).

The process of discernment is helpful since it presents a positive outlook on engaging with material rather than necessarily having a definitive answer to its meaning.[5] In this way, it relates very well to what I have spoken of at the beginning of this section about the ordinary human experience of trying to understand things. Very rarely can I say that I understand something completely; I am always picking up new clues about something or seeing something from an angle where I had not positioned myself before. What discernment has to offer to the hermeneutical process is the intentional application of my understanding to my ordinary life experience. The hermeneutical and discernment processes together comprise a process of insight that relates to the whole experience of a person.

THE HERMENEUTICAL PROCESS

At this point, I want to introduce a process—explaining it step by step—that you might use in approaching any material for study. I will then present a case study to outline how these steps might work in practice.

The process has four key steps:

1. describing the phenomenon in its context;
2. describing your own standpoint;
3. understanding the phenomenon;
4. taking a position: academic and personal accountability.

You should not see these steps as linear, going from 1 to 4 and finishing there, but rather as a continuum on which you will constantly move backward and forward among steps 2, 3, and 4.

As I outline the steps, you may wish to practice the process by choosing and working on one experience or some material that you consider religious in nature that is related to women's experience in some way. It may be helpful to start in a space that is familiar to you, culturally, geographically, temporally, and religiously. Starting from what you know best may alert you to your own blind spots with something that is very close to you.

Step 1: Describing the Phenomenon in Its Context

In step 1, you gather your first impressions of the material you want to analyze and understand. Some of the impressions you have at this stage will be addressed in more detail as you undertake step 3. At this early stage, try to describe the phenomenon in as broad a context as possible and in as many different ways as possible—the sensory perceptions, the intellectual perceptions, the patterns that seem obvious, the overall impression, the individual elements that seem to stand out more than others, and so on. How is this phenomenon speaking to you, in how many different ways, from how many different angles?

Step 2: Describing Your Own Standpoint

In carrying out step 2, you move your focus of attention from the material to yourself. Like step 1, step 2 is only an introductory step, and you will come back to these questions again and again as you engage the material for study. For example, this second question—about where you are standing—should be asked often during the entire process, since your standpoint will change as you go further and further into your study.

At this stage, you try to describe your own particular context as carefully as you can. Some possible questions to help you do this are as follows:

- Where am I standing to listen to, describe, and understand this particular material?
- What is the background that I bring to this listening and analytical exercise—my race, culture, gender, and so on?
- If this material comes from a particular religious tradition, am I a believer, former believer, interested onlooker? Does this material speak to me on an intellectual/believing/feeling/spiritual/aesthetic level—or a combination of these?
- What has prepared me in the past for this study?
- Where have my questions about this material come from (life questions and scientific questions)?
- Am I prepared to be open to the possibility that my questions may change as I undertake the study?

Step 3: Understanding the Phenomenon

Step 3 is the intellectual core of the process, the place where the hard slog of thinking and analyzing and reflection is carried out. Some of the questions to ask yourself at this stage are as follows:

- According to my background in intellectual life, what kinds of pattern and paradigm do I have the ability to bring to this particular material—that is, am I a student of women's studies or a student of comparative religion or a drama/architecture/literature/medical/... student?

- What further reading do I need to do to understand possible paradigms for contextualizing some aspect of this particular phenomenon?
- Of all the methods and paradigms familiar to me (sociological, historical, psychological, text critical, etc.), which method or combination of methods will suit this material, will distort it least, will give sufficient space for the richness of the material?
- What new questions have occurred to me since I began my study of this phenomenon? Do these new questions indicate a need to change the kind of method I am using or to add another method to the combination I am already using?

As I work with the material and go through the intellectual engagement with it, I note what kinds of feelings may be surfacing or in the background—whether these be feelings of satisfaction at being able to understand or grasp some aspect of the material, feelings of frustration at not being able to fully grasp how one might get the best out of it or interpret it, revulsion at what is happening or being described, or feelings of well-being that the material finds some resonating point in my own being. Although this section on method is more focused on intellectual ability, this particular point about feelings is important. If I am aware of my feelings, I can be more alert to their influence on my interpretation of the data and to what that implies for a richer or a more limited interpretation. If my feelings are very strong, then I need to be careful that they do not overwhelm my intellectual engagement with the material but, rather, inform this engagement in a balanced way.

The method of preparing to interpret involves a number of levels. First, I need to listen to primary material where people tell/sing/dance/paint/mold/. . . their own stories or the events in which they have been involved. If this primary material comes from a culture or religion other than my own, I am already interpreting across cultures or across different religious experience as I listen. I will also need to consult secondary material where people report and/or analyze what others have said in their own stories or descriptions. These will be useful for gathering information to prepare myself for interpreting or for checking my responses against what others have said.

Step 4: Taking a Position: Academic and Personal Accountability

By the hermeneutical process that I have outlined above, I am hoping for an outcome both academically/intellectually and personally accountable. The discernment model by which I learn to differentiate implies also that I make some judgment that is in keeping with the kinds of values I hold and that finds its basis in a cooperation between the head and the heart. If I engage the material to the fullest extent of which I am capable, then both my mind and heart are engaged, and I make a judgment either explicitly or implicitly. I cannot really avoid the way in which I will be psychologically involved, the way in which I will have feelings about what I see or listen to, so my stance both throughout and at the conclusion of the process cannot be neutral.

This final step of the process demands some hard thinking about ethics. Above all, an ethics is called for that is both pragmatic and practical. Throughout the process, I have asked you to be aware of yourself and of your various personal reactions to the material studied as well as to the intellectual analyses being made. I have both positive and negative reactions to material. Positive reactions can present difficulties such as a possible overidentification with the material, which I need to be aware of. However, I may stand in a particular place to listen to the phenomenon, in which I may feel some resistance to or unease with the material. The discernment process demands that I be honest about the unease and how that shapes my opinion or judgment about the material.

An uneasy or negative response to material must not be hidden away, but neither must it be aggressively presented. A considered, reasoned, and respectful response, even when negative, can set a sure groundwork for dialogue with those whose experience I have listened to. In this way, I learn to distinguish between a genuine respect and a disingenuous permissiveness that allows for everything except speaking the truth about my intellectual and personal judgments. If those whose experience I have listened to do not agree with me, their opinions need to be heard as other perspectives (no matter what their own beliefs about the authority of their statements within a particular culture or religious tradition). What matters is the quality of engagement with those with whom I disagree, and the reader must always be willing to be engaged, with the possibility that questions and opinions may change in that engagement. In the end, it is my behavior that makes the difference to the outcome of dialogue.[6]

AN EXAMPLE OF THE HERMENEUTICAL PROCESS

Having outlined the hermeneutical process, I move on to a case study to demonstrate that process at work. In keeping with what I suggested for you in the first section, the case study focuses on a phenomenon related to women's religious experience from a context very familiar to me. The phenomenon I have chosen is a book by Richard Leonard entitled *Beloved Daughters: 100 Years of Papal Teaching on Women* (1995).[7]

Step 1: Describing the Phenomenon in Its Context

TEXT AND CONTEXT. *Beloved Daughters* is a small volume by Richard Leonard, an Australian Jesuit priest, part of his Masters of Theology dissertation for the Melbourne College of Divinity. I knew of Leonard's work even before the book appeared, since many women, including me, who were involved in theological work in Australia at the time were aware that Leonard had been studying feminist theology and had gone on to do postgraduate work in that area. He must have been one of the first, if not *the* first, male cleric to undertake postgraduate studies in feminist theology in Australia.

The first three chapters of Leonard's book give the primary

material about women in the last hundred years of papal documents, with an emphasis on two recent documents from John Paul
II: *Mulieris dignitatem* (On the Dignity of Women) and *Ordinatio
sacerdotalis* (Priestly Ordination). The chapters following those
first three provide a number of things: an overview of positive and
negative reactions by commentators to the teaching (mostly of
Mulieris dignitatem); a study and comparison of papal hermeneutics (Cardinal Ratzinger as representative of the papal hermeneutic with regard to scripture) with the hermeneutics of the feminist biblical scholar Elisabeth Schüssler Fiorenza; a presentation
of the difficulties in the papal teaching (especially John Paul II's)
about the vocation of women; an appeal to take the papal documents on their own terms and to continue the dialogue; and a
warning about disintegration within the church if there is no dialogue.

Various contexts within which to read this small volume include
the following:

- the history of papal statements and the levels of authority
  attributed to different types of statements;
- the context of the author within the Society of Jesus (Jesuit
  priests)—a group of male religious professionals within the
  Catholic church;
- the Australian context in which this volume appears, where
  there is a groundswell of criticism of the Vatican stance on
  the question of women's ordination to the priesthood even
  while there is an increasing emphasis on "no dialogue"
  from the Vatican.

Step 2: Describing Your Standpoint

ACADEMIC STANDPOINT. I first read this book in response to a request
for a review for an Australian journal of Studies in Religion.[8] In
this instance, I approached the book as a person who teaches
Studies in Religion (including a class on women and religion) in
the Australian secular university context. It would provide a source
of information for my teaching, since many students either have

a background in Catholicism or are simply interested in the kinds
of influential statements made by the Vatican.

PERSONAL AND COMMUNITY STANDPOINT. I was also interested in the
book (and I suspect the book was given to me to review) because
I was at the time a member of a Catholic women's religious order and had tried to keep up with the range of recent writings of
Catholic feminist theologians and papal/Vatican statements relating to women's religious experience.

From my experience of the recent history of papal pronouncements relating to women, I had strong reservations—even
before I began—about the possibility for reasoned and enlightened debate. I was certainly interested in the material but also
loath to put myself once more in a position where I would probably be angry and disheartened by what I read. It was an effort to
try to be open, to be prepared that Leonard might have a new
perspective that would prove constructive or that he might report
on another's work that could be helpful. I was aware that intellectual questions and probings would go hand in hand with strong
feelings about the text.

My initial questions were both academic and personal, asking,
first, how well Leonard had succeeded in his critical task, and second, how possible it might be for a male celibate cleric to really
appreciate the position of women now and previously in the
church and to offer something that might be helpful to my current experience.

Step 3: Understanding the Phenomenon

Presenting a case study of a book has its own difficulties for those
who do not have access to it unless a great deal of detail is included. Since this is out of the question here, I have taken one
section of material from the book that is well in keeping with the
tenor of the whole work and given an idea of my processing of
that section. There is a theme and argument concerning the place
and role of women that runs like a thread through a number of
the papal statements, and it is this that I have addressed, begin-

ning with some of the simpler material and working through to
the more complex.

My first action was to take a quick look through the text, noting how Leonard organized his material under various chapter
headings, dipping very quickly into a page here and there, looking at the kinds of books that appear in the bibliography. Even if
I had not been sure from the title of the book what a reading
might entail, after this first quick impression I had some idea of
questions and paradigms through which I could begin critically
examining and forming an opinion on the book, from areas as diverse as theology, women's studies, church history, sociology, and
hermeneutics. I knew some approaches would eventually be more
helpful than others, but this kind of decision can be made only
within the process of trying various questions on the material.

NEVER JUDGE A BOOK BY ITS COVER? To be honest, my very first impression and first reactions were to the cover of the book. The
cover shows a woman, a detail from a depiction of the annunci-
ation of the angel Gabriel to Mary. At first glance, I took it to depict a woman biting her nails in worry or perplexity, the picture
of a very tentative woman. I was aware that this is possibly a true
way of depicting how some women have felt about some of their
experiences in the Catholic Church, but I wondered why Leonard
(or the publisher) had chosen this picture instead of a more positive and strong portrayal of women, given that I knew quite a few
women would be interested in reading Leonard's work.

TWO STATEMENTS ABOUT WOMEN, THEIR STATUS, AND THEIR RIGHTS.
Early in the book, Leonard gives the example of a papal document (*Mulieris dignitatem*) that supports the position that women
and men do not have equal rights in marriage: The married
woman must be obedient to her husband. The document then
goes on to say that if a woman wanted equal rights, it would mean
that she would have to demean herself, to come down from her
truly regal throne and her status of rational and exalted liberty.
I was unsure what the status of "rational liberty" might be but took
the statement to be presenting a scenario in which a woman could

be simultaneously the one who is obedient to another and the one who rules as queen and is free.

A little further on, there is a very similar argument, this time in relation to priestly ordination rather than to marriage. Leonard presents a document (*Ordinatio sacerdotalis*) that initially seems to support the equality of men and women. However, we read further that women are higher than men by virtue of the fact that they have a womb and thus mirror God the creator. If women demand the same rights as men with regard to priestly ordination, they will be lowering themselves from their superior status.

The document also tells us that only men can be ordained because "their maleness establishes a clear and unambiguous link with the *persona Christi*." If this statement characterizes women/ femaleness by the symbol of the womb, then I supposed that "maleness" should be interpreted as referring to the symbol of male genitalia. I took the statement to be saying, in fact, that women and men are not equal; their essential difference and relative position are constituted by a hierarchy of power based on different physical sexual characteristics, which symbolize their standing in relation to divine activity. The statement also seemed to say that the creator God is greater than the risen Christ and thus that women are of higher status than men.

Questions About the Logic of the Statements. At this stage, I wanted to ask some very simple questions with regard to the logic of the statements and the line of argument. How could it be demeaning for a woman to want equal rights in marriage or in priestly ministry? Is she not already demeaned by being told that she must be obedient to her husband or that she is not capable of mirroring the risen Christ in a clear and unambiguous way so as to be eligible for priestly ordination (even though she is like God)?[9]

The discrepancy in the first description between having a higher status and being at the same time in a position of obedience to another is clear. Perhaps the same kind of discrepancy is not clear in the second description. It could be a simple statement about biological difference, implying that one lesser role in the church was not available to women because of their biological makeup but that other roles of higher status were available to them. Certainly, I am told that women have a higher status by virtue of having a womb. However, some knowledge about the relative status of official roles in the Catholic church and the history of its clerical hierarchy, together with my personal experience of the church at the grass-roots level, indicates that the clerical expert/priest (and all the levels of priesthood thereafter including bishop and pope) has a position of authority and power second to none. Knowing this, the discrepancy in the second description is clear.

There is a further inconsistency in that although woman mirrors God because of her womb and man mirrors Christ because of his maleness, God is not said to be female, nor his creative activity sexual, while it is implied that the risen Christ is male in the same sense that men are male in the context of this world. One type of mirroring by virtue of physiological features is taken metaphorically and the other literally. At this stage, I am into an area of symbolic language that requires expertise in the philosophy of language.

Questions About the Definition of Persons in the Statements: Biology. The first thing that seemed obvious about the statements was that they attempt to put together a number of disparate areas: some theological concepts about the relationship of God and Christ to human beings with an added concern for the hierarchy of power in both of these relational elements, biological concepts about the basic identification of human beings into male and female, and an (implicit) political/biological concept about the rights of males only to be ordained ministers. Any of these aspects would be suitable for further investigation, using models and questions from theology and church history as a possible starting point. However, in this case, I chose to look at the sorts of gender assumptions that are being made, and the way in which biology is being used as a basis for doing theology, to define something essential about men and women in relation to God and Christ.

Thus, I interpreted each of the arguments to present women and men basically in terms of the symbolic focus of their repro-

ductive capacity; that is, woman = womb and man = male genitalia. Interestingly, only the woman's reproductive capacity is explicitly part of the further equation as it moves into the area of
theology: A woman is like God because of her creative activity
(i.e., in this case, creativity is defined in terms of sexual creative
activity in reproduction). When the equation about a man is taken
into the realm of theology, there is no statement about reproductive activity but rather one about how a man's maleness provides the link with Christ's maleness, and this relates to power in
ritual, sexuality as power, and gender as criterion for the person
who may be allowed to preside at a ritual that, in the popular
Catholic consciousness (but in poor theological terms), creates
the presence of the (presumably male) risen Christ.

Questions About the Definition of Persons: Theology. At first sight, the
two arguments about rights in marriage and about the right to
ordination did not seem to be connected apart from the common suggestion that women would lower themselves if they were
to struggle for equal rights in these areas. However, the two are
connected in that what makes a woman queen is her likeness (by
biology) to Mary; that is, papal statements laud Mary as the
supreme example of womanhood, and she is Queen of Heaven
as the mother of Christ, who is God. What forms the bond between Mary and other women, according to the papal statements,
is their mutual possession of a womb. Thus, the primary equation
is woman/Mary = womb (used [mother] or unused [virgin]).
What makes Mary different and unique is the fact that she is described as the virgin mother (a womb used and unused at the
same time).[10]

Questions About Symbolic Language. This difficulty with the literal
or metaphorical understanding of symbolic language occurs frequently in the statements and leads time and again to confusion.
Mulieris dignitatem states, for example, that female imagery used
for the church, especially the church as Bride of Christ, is inappropriate if interpreted literally because men are part of the
church membership and they would feel excluded in such an in-

terpretation. No such difficulty is identified by the document where male imagery for the risen Christ is taken literally so that only males may represent the risen Christ clearly and unambiguously, an interpretation that effectively sidelines women from clear and unambiguous representation in the body of the risen Christ.

Questions About Critical Analysis and Hermeneutics of the Author: Context and Personal Standpoint. None of this receives any critical analysis from Leonard, and thus I supposed that he had not recognized one of the most important bases of the statements. That he had not became even clearer in the few pages of the conclusion. On pages 58 to 60, Leonard suggests that the whole crux for current debate in the church is the issue of women's vocation, since recent papal statements recognize the equality of women and men and request that women be able to play their part fully in all spheres of life "according to their own particular nature." From my analysis so far, I questioned that the church had indeed recognized the equality of women and men, given its view of the "particular nature" of a woman. My conclusion was that it is not vocation that is the crux but the very understanding of woman/femaleness.

The serious lack of critical work in the text brought me to reflect on the whole aspect of a Catholic male professional writing a book about papal statements on women and on the broader issue within religious groups of the generally justifying role of religious experts versus the challenging role of prophetic members.

Step 4: Taking a Position

I have given one small example of a section in the text and how I approached it through a variety of questions about logic, church history and organization, gender analysis, and philosophy of language as well as aspects of my personal experience and knowledge as a believer. I could not really do justice to all the concerns of the text and the variety of models and questions that should be brought to bear on it, such as the sociological models of the life and maintenance of religious groups or the ecclesiological model presumed by the author.

I have done my critical work on the primary texts and Leonard's commentary. I think that I understand some of the underlying bases of both, or, at least, I have put some questions about what that might be. At this stage, I am ready to move to another level of reflection, to an overarching reflection on voices, a level that I have touched upon only briefly in the third section.

Whose voice do I hear in this book? The first voice that I hear is the voice of the papacy. Do I hear women's voices? If so, which women?

Leonard's example suggests that male professionals of the institutional church may speak for women and speak about what women are. He characterizes this process as using the long line of apostolic continuity and interpretation to make its statements *within the whole Christian community.* He reiterates the word "whole" in relation to the Christian community three times. *Mulieris dignitatem* "is retelling the story of the Christian church in relation to the particular situation of women, drawing on the whole community's experience and reflection on the life of Jesus and the example of Mary."[11] We will return to this idea of the institution that speaks for and about women in chapter 3.

Two women's voices are heard in the text, Elizabeth Johnson in the foreword and Elisabeth Schüssler Fiorenza in the section on feminist hermeneutics. Which other women speak in the text? Those who have no voice but are represented are women who are mothers and virgins.

Where are the men's voices? Who does Leonard speak for when he says "we"? The men by and large are the expert male professionals. There is little mention of nonclerical laymen.

Leonard concludes his book with a plea for dialogue between feminist hermeneutics and papal hermeneutics. What is Leonard's perception of the dialogue process? Who are the partners? Where is the dialogue situated? If the dialogue fails or does not take place, what are the consequences for each party? And who will be held responsible?

The dialogue Leonard envisages between the Vatican and fem-

inist scholarship is not an equal dialogue, so it may be inappropriate to use the term *dialogue*, which presupposes some kind of
equal partnership in the process. If the dialogue breaks down, the
losers in terms of power within the church will be the feminists,
since Leonard's scenario for breakdown is of schism between an
official and an unoffical church. The official church, the papacy—
the Vatican—will remain. The onus is on the feminists to want
and continue the dialogue. So, one dialogue partner cannot
"lose," no matter what happens.

CONCLUSION

I would ask you at this stage to note the different methods used
in the case study, how the study demonstrates that the breadth of
the material offers a variety of challenges for interpretation and
understanding and calls for corresponding varieties of questions
and methods.

Having seen the variety and depth of the questions that I have
needed to ask in the process of doing the case study, it should be
clear that Studies in Religion has no discipline discrete to itself
but needs to call on a breadth of disciplines such as history, sociology, anthropology, literary criticism, philosophy, and theology.

In the next chapter, I move from the case study that deals with
a specific phenomenon that is relatively familiar to me to a
broader canvas of religious groups and the situation of women
within these groups.

NOTES

1. Pierre Wolff, *Discernment: The Art of Choosing Well* (Ligouri, Mo.:
Triumph Books, 1993), p. 3.

2. Wolff, *Discernment*, pp. 4–7.

3. Wolff, *Discernment*, p. 5.

4. Wolff, *Discernment*, p. 6.

5. Suzanne G. Farnham et al., *Listening Hearts: Discerning Call in Community* (Harrisburg, Pa.: Morehouse, 1991), p. 26.

6. I was pleased to see the same regard for women as subjects of lively dialogue summed up succinctly in Maura O'Neill's *Women Speaking, Women Listening: Women in Interreligious Dialogue* (Maryknoll, N.Y.: Orbis Books, 1990).

7. Richard Leonard, *Beloved Daughters: 100 Years of Papal Teaching on Women* (Melbourne: David Lovell, 1995).

8. Majella Franzmann, "'Cast yourselves recklessly into the current of life!' A Critical Response to Richard Leonard's *Beloved Daughters: 100 Years of Papal Teaching on Women*," *Australian Religion Studies Review*, vol. 8/2 (1995), pp. 104–8.

9. I use the term *risen* deliberately here since the argument is focused on the ability of men to preside at the Catholic eucharistic ritual in which the risen Christ is said to be present. There is no difficulty in affirming the literal maleness of the historical human being, the Jew Jesus of Nazareth, who, after his death, is proclaimed by Christians as the risen Christ.

10. The term *virgin* is taken in a literal biological sense, unlike the title "virgin mother" applied to other Near Eastern goddesses, who are clearly not virgins in the literal physical sense.

11. Leonard, *Beloved Daughters*, p. 73.

2

Learning Languages — A Context for Reading and Writing About Religion and Women

—ഡ—

In chapter 1, I outlined a hermeneutical process for analyzing material from the general area of women and religion. Where this material is relatively familiar to you, you may not experience much difficulty in setting it in a context. Difficulties may begin to emerge when you have material including aspects of women's experience of religion that may be quite unfamiliar to you. In such a case, the task is to come as close to the material as you can: to get as much information as is available to you; to critique this information, its sources, and its perspective; and to contextualize this material accurately and respectfully. All this takes place while you are aware of perhaps an extreme difference between the account of the women's experience and your own experience. I have already dealt with this issue to some extent in the introduction.

Just as I cannot extrapolate from one woman's experience to a generic "women's experience," so can I not extrapolate for all women from one woman's religious experience, whether across traditions or within a particular tradition. Thus, the experience of a Buddhist woman in China will not be the same as the experience of a Buddhist woman in Sri Lanka; Christian women will have different experiences in Chile or in Australia or in Poland; Muslim women's lives will be different in Iran and in Germany. Even all Chinese Buddhist women will not have the same experience, nor all Christian Chilean women, nor Muslim German women. Treating the experiences of women from different periods of history makes the situation even more complex.

As a first step in facing this kind of difficulty, in this chapter I suggest some starting points for reflecting on the breadth of experience that will be represented in the material available to you for study. I will concentrate first on the term *religion* and then widen the discussion to include women's experience within religious groups, religious definitions of women, the issue of identity in relation to the variety of religious traditions, and some women's definitions or critiques of religion.

LANGUAGE ABOUT RELIGION

The Term Religion

The word *religion* comes from the Latin *religio*, which probably (though scholars are not certain) comes from the verb *religare*, which means "to bind again." The term was used in ancient Rome to describe the activity of citizens in offering public honor in rituals to the gods and goddesses of the state. The concept of binding may refer then to the relationship between the deities and the state as well as to the relationship of citizen to citizen within their activity as a community of worshippers.

In current popular usage, the term religion can have a much broader meaning—groups of believers associated together within an organized system of belief (e.g., "world religions" or "the Jewish religion") or an individual experience of some sacred or extraordinary reality (e.g., "she got religion" or "she has become very religious"). The Latin term in its original usage relates really only to the first example, in which religion is situated within communities, cultures, or sections of cultures—though not everyone within a particular culture need be religious or self-identify as religious.

From the point of view of the outsider (nonpractitioner), a religion is a social organization with rituals, stories, structures, laws, and activities that can be observed and described. For the insider (member) of a religious group, such observations can only record external details. Other purposes of religious affiliation may be invisible. For example, believers may experience religious feelings of awe, devotion, and fear, or they may have a personal relationship with a sacred power, or they may experience a union with such a power, or they may go through various stages and degrees of uncertainty about their belief in a sacred power. Both the externally observable phenomena and the personal experience, which cannot be observed but only described by the believer, are part of what I call religion.

There is little consensus among scholars about what constitutes religion, but you will find that many scholarly definitions emphasize a personal or social reaction or behavior to define what religion is. The real question, however, is what it is that groups or individuals are reacting to. Religion is certainly concerned with behaviors, but it also has concepts about what inspires the behaviors or "drives" them. Generally speaking, what drives religious systems and their various activities and beliefs is some concept of a power or extraordinary reality, whether this be perceived as transcendent to (moving above/beyond) or immanent in (moving within) the world. In using the words "power" and "reality," I am not implying necessarily any kind of personal deity or deities but, rather, allowing for a full range of options including the extraordinary reality of *nirvana* (enlightenment) experienced by some Buddhists. Of course, people are religious for a variety of reasons, and this general definition may not adequately sum up even the core value of a religion for all believers.

Religious experience covers a vast range of behaviors. I have already mentioned experience with a power or extraordinary reality that results in feelings of awe, devotion, union, and uncertainty. But religious experience is not limited to an individual's personal experience with deity or an extraordinary reality. Many textbooks on religious experience give the mistaken impression that "real" religious experience is limited to some kind of mystical or ascetical behavior. This is only one possible understanding. Religious activity does not need to be extreme (in a physical, psychological, or spiritual way) to be labeled "religious." For many believers, religious experience is, above all, what occurs within the activity of a community, whether that be in some kind of worship setting or in much more ordinary activity. This point will become important later when I consider the predominantly domestic or communal nature of many women's religious activity.

Believers within an organized system of belief do not necessarily use the term *religion* to describe what their group is or does. Sometimes scholars refer to the Sanskrit term *dharma* as the word in Hinduism that comes closest to the English term religion. Dharma is variously translated as "truth," "duty," "law," "order," and "right." It refers to the way in which a believer conforms to the laws and duties and conventions of the social order, which itself is based on the laws that govern the cosmic order. The Buddhist Pali term related to it is *dhamma.* This term has a stronger emphasis on doctrine than the Hindu word. Dhamma is based in the teachings of the Buddha, especially as they are summed up in the Four Excellent Truths and the Excellent Eightfold Path. Interestingly, the word *yoga* means "to bind" or "to yoke" in the sense of binding the believer to the sacred power. In one sense, this term may be seen as closer than dharma to the term religion since it uses the image of binding to a deity. On the other hand, yoga does not have the connotation of binding one believer to another or to the group of believers, which dharma may cover in its concern for ethically and socially ordered relationships.

In this book, I will not be discussing the nature or actual existence of such a power or reality. I respect the views of believers that it exists and forms the focus of their various religious systems. In saying this, I do not mean to imply that if such a power or extraordinary reality exists, it is only mediated or accessed by religious systems or wholly defined by those who attempt to name it with religious language.

This concept of a power or extraordinary reality gives rise to a number of important questions. How can I speak about such a power? How can I use human language and imagery for it? How can I communicate with it or relate to it without perishing in the attempt? How can I take cognizance of this power and yet remain in a relatively normal relationship to the everyday world? These are some of the important questions that any religious group attempts to answer for its members—and questions also that individuals might attempt to answer for themselves.

In the next section, I move to consider the organizational/social dimensions of religious groups and women's experience within them. There are many models under which I could categorize the variety of religious groups. For example, I could characterize the kinds of religious behaviors that one could observe—whether uninhibitedly ecstatic or highly formalized. I have chosen to use the categories of religious groups in relation to different sociocultural settings. Different sociocultural perceptions of women and their experience are key factors in how religious groups see women in their context and give a role to them. Religious systems cannot operate in a vacuum outside of cultural expression and language.

The Experience of Women in Religious Groups

WOMEN IN NATURAL RELIGIOUS COMMUNITIES. I am using the description "natural religious community" for the situation in which a particular culture and religion are coterminous; that is, a separate religious identity does not exist, what I would call religion is totally integrated into the life-experience of the group, and there is a unified sociocultural identity that permeates all experience. Sometimes the term *primal* is used to describe the religious life of such groups.

In these groups, the religious function of the member is bound totally to the whole life of the community. In Australia, such a situation would have existed within indigenous aboriginal groups before white European invasion. An aboriginal woman would have had only one cultural "map," which would have included and integrated her religious experience: It would have traced her experience of the Dreaming, her marriage, her diet, her hunting techniques, and so on.

In the current world, such a community is rare, existing only where geographic isolation is still possible or where a group has isolated itself intentionally. Thus, it is necessary to make the important distinction between the closed systems of religious experience within small-scale forager or village societies and the majority of religions, sometimes called expansionist, universalizing, or universal religions, which will be dealt with in the following chapters.

Of course, there will be cases where the categories overlap to some extent. What I identify as Hinduism belongs to a natural religious community, for one is born into Hinduism; and yet it has been exported in a number of ways to other communities, both Eastern and Western. I am thinking here not only of Hare Krishna devotees in my own country but also of the strong Hindu influence to be found in even strongly Buddhist countries like Thailand.

As cultural isolation becomes less and less possible for groups, natural religious communities will have to negotiate changes in their identity with the wider culture or become extinct. Forcibly colonized and converted (to Christianity), Australian aboriginal people are today creating new religious identities in response to their wider multicultural environment and to the revival of aboriginal interest in their traditional religion and culture. An indigenous woman in Australia today may be Christian while also often fully integrating her aboriginal spirituality within her religious life.

In the chapters that follow, I will not be including natural religious communities in the discussion to any great extent. The religious experience and participation of women in small-scale forager and village societies are too diverse and different to be included in the broad generalizations that I will draw from the state-based institutionalized religions and their similar structures.

WOMEN IN UNIVERSALIZING RELIGIOUS COMMUNITIES. The universalizing (or universal) religious group is not contained within a particular culture, race, or geographic location but moves across boundaries and encounters a variety of sociocultural and political situations as well as other religions. Where the boundaries between the wider world and the group are quite permeable, the wider community provides a constant frame of reference and a potential partner in discussion. In this environment, religious identity is a subset of other overlapping identities for the individual members of the group, and members will differ with regard to political affiliation or cultural and ethnic background. There are women who identify themselves as Muslim who are Indonesian, African, Palestinian, English, or German, and there are women who are Jewish who regard that as a religious identity and other women who are Jewish who regard that as a secular ethnic identity.

While the universalizing group is not contained in any particular location or group of people, the experience of most people within a tradition or religious group is local; that is, the people are concerned for the most part with the activities of a group in a limited geographic area despite the fact that there may be broader concerns in the group for communication or learning or aid work or missionary activity on an international scale.

In the introduction to this chapter, I spoke of the difference in experience of a Buddhist woman in China and a Buddhist woman in Sri Lanka. Categorizing certain religions as universalizing does not mean that they will manifest themselves in exactly the same way in whatever location they are found. There is always a vast variety within any tradition, influenced by a two-way process of the religion adapting to the cultural setting and receiving cultural and folk accretions in return. Because of this, I prefer to speak of Christianities, Buddhisms, Islams, and so on rather than Christianity, Buddhism, and Islam. In relation to women, then, this means that where women are limited by aspects of a particular culture or folk system, those aspects may also have their effect eventually within the religious tradition, or perhaps the religious tradition will include such aspects from the very beginning.

Some traditions put great emphasis on the location in which the tradition arose. Although there is a clear advantage for practitioners to understand the culture in which their religion originated, there is no guarantee that the religion that continues in this place is closest to what the founder or founding group intended it to be. Neither closeness in geographic location nor closeness in time is any guarantee of some greater purity of the tradition. Thus, a Christian Palestinian woman living in first century CE Judaea would not necessarily be any closer to living an authentic Christian life than a Christian Chilean woman now.

Despite the limited arena of activity in a local situation, how membership is understood in the group may ultimately rest with authorities on the international level, whether that be through some formalized and integrated network of the highest ranking religious professionals for the group (such as the central bureaucracy of the Roman Catholic division of Christianity in the Vatican), or through a council of professionals who come together from local groups (such as the various Buddhist, Islamic, or Jewish councils), or through the more subtle or indirect influence from powerful individual groups themselves in a limited geographic area (such as the influence of Saudi Arabia on Muslims, either through its financial support for projects in a number of Muslim-majority countries or in the values and ideas imbibed by those who come to Saudi Arabia as migrant workers[1]).

International control of policy and practice in overt or covert ways may produce a very limited view of membership in any religious tradition. Where contemporary or even historical texts are controlled by a political and religious elite, large groups of people in various populations who lack any access to these texts or any means of creating and disseminating documents of their own within the tradition may simply remain invisible. Thus, the lower orders of society are virtually invisible in the texts of the Brahmins, who represent the highest caste within Hinduism. Western Christian texts are still generally Eurocentric, with little interest in Christians of Eastern or nonwhite cultural heritage. And women simply do not figure in most texts from universalizing religious traditions.

Religions that set a high store on community or on inner cohesiveness through international control may use the concept of the necessity of this community itself in attempts to force a certain view of membership, which may be under question by smaller groups within the community. Thus, within the debate about women's ordination in the Anglican church, many male Anglican professionals warned that to question the assigned identity of women in this way would cause a schism; that is, women would be responsible for the breakup of the entire group. At the same time, other professionals within the Roman Catholic church warned that ordaining Anglican women would set back the cause of church unity between Anglican and Roman Catholic groups. Karma Lekshe Tsomo writes of a similar phenomenon in Buddhism, relating how a Sri Lankan ordained monk charged that creating a system of ordained Buddhist nuns would be equivalent to causing a schism in the global Buddhist community, which is a serious offense.[2]

Universalizing religious groups that have strong numbers globally may not only make policy for their own membership but try also to influence political and social policy making that affects nonmembers. This can be seen in the current heated debates about the right to voluntary euthanasia or abortion, or about gay rights, or in the rather uniform international language about so-called "cults." The phenomenon is not new and, when wedded to systems of power in which women have little place or regard, can be particularly oppressive.

One significant example is found in Victorian England, a society in which women had few rights as individuals even with regard to access to the law. In the 1840s, Miss Louisa Nottidge, a wealthy middle-aged spinster, left her home to follow a charismatic sect leader, Henry Prince, the "Beloved," as three of her sisters had previously done. Prince had founded a millenarian community in Somerset based on teachings about free love and everlasting life. He demanded that followers bequeath their possessions to the community. With her fourth daughter at risk of doing so, Mrs. Nottidge had Louisa abducted with the help of a male relative and confined in an asylum in London on the grounds of monomania with religious delusions. When Louisa was finally released, she proceeded to sue for wrongful detention. The Lord Chief Baron dismissed the defense's case that she had been saved from a "class of persons who entertained certain peculiar notions upon religion," saying that he doubted whether any man, or even a married woman in a similar situation, would have been so mishandled. Alex Owen comments: "Nothing could have been more clear than this final observation that it was women, and in particular those who lacked a sympathetic husband, who stood in the greatest danger of unwarranted incarceration."[3]

That married women should also have been included in the comments is borne out by the subsequent experience of Mrs. Louisa Lowe, a spiritualist, who was confined to an asylum by order of her husband, the Reverend Lowe, in 1870 despite a doctor's self-proclaimed inability to pronounce her insane, and was only permitted to leave when her husband made a premature bid to get his hands on her money.[4] Although there was much else at stake in each of these incidents, particularly economic matters, the basis of the action by the perpetrators was said to be the religious belief or activity of the women.

The examples above concern the disquiet of Christian believers or a Christian-influenced society with new forms of religious belief and practice and the assignment of negative identity or a Christian nonidentity to them. That there were other factors at play is not at all surprising. The assignment of nonidentity or a negative identity is rarely, if ever, contained within a purely theological discussion. The process of assigning negative identity may gain its impetus from the simple fact of the mainstream religious institution's having been bypassed as a place in which the new religious group wishes to situate itself. The subsequent perceived loss of power or loss of face by the mainstream organization may cause it to move against the smaller group.

This can be illustrated from the experience of the Beguines (and their male counterparts, the Beghards) in thirteenth-century Belgium and Holland. The Beguines were groups of unmarried women who tried to live in simplicity according to their understanding of how the earliest Christian communities lived, adopting radical poverty but without the structure of a vowed, enclosed convent life. The Christian church pressured them to join or associate themselves with recognized religious orders, and many subsequently did so, especially attaching themselves to the religious order of the Dominicans. But those who decided to remain outside of the church's official structures for religious groups were often hunted down as heretics. One of the most famous is Marguerite Porete, who was burned at the stake in 1310. Her book, *Mirror of Simple Souls* (burned sometime prior to her own burning), advocated a teaching of "Free Spirit" that challenged the authority of the Christian church in a number of ways. She attacked the notion of an ordained clergy and their learned status (which could not guarantee their understanding of mystical experience), argued against the necessity of sacramental ministry, and proposed that a greater authority was to be found in lives of poverty, purity, and evangelism.[5]

WOMEN WITHIN SECTARIAN RELIGIOUS COMMUNITIES. Sectarian groups are generally local, with little or no reference to the wider world. I would characterize many current sectarian groups as manifesting a type of isolationist fundamentalism. Sectarian religious groups, moreover, are generally "world denying," either with an indifferent attitude to the world or a stance against the world. Thus, these groups keep themselves separate as far as possible, either physically or ideologically, from the dominant cultural context in which they find themselves. Where the boundaries between the world and the group are drawn strictly, group cohesion is usually extremely high, with a high level of rhetoric against the powers of this world. The major focus of such groups is the salvation or holiness of group members.

It might be expected that women would have reasonable status and equal access to salvation in these groups, especially where they have little or no status in the cultural world that is being denied. However, there is no guarantee that this will be the case. In first-century CE Palestine, for example, it is possible to see two sectarian groups within Judaism—the Jesus sect and the Qumran sect—with very different attitudes to the role of women. In the former (at least during the lifetime of the sect founder, Jesus of Nazareth), there seems to have been a relatively liberal attitude in allowing women access to the key role of disciple, while in the latter, the elite core group of the Sons of Light was made up of celibate males.

Often, the very structures of the powers against which the group is protesting are themselves found in operation in the group. There may even be a more oppressive structure for women, given the closed and strictly cohesive nature of the group and the way in which the power structure of the group is supported and validated by cosmic powers.

The Functions of Women and Their Place Within the Structures of Religious Groups

In this section, I outline the various functions and roles in which women are engaged in religious groups in their public institutional life. I deal with certain issues in relation to these functions and roles in more detail in the following chapters.

THE LAYWOMAN. By far the most common function and role of women in religious groups is that of the nonprofessional female believer, the "ordinary" believer, who together with nonprofessional men makes up the bulk of the membership. These are the people who have no particular designated authority or role that sets them in any way apart from or above the other members. Religious power and meaning are mediated to them by the skill and knowledge of the religious professionals.

Very often in this capacity, women are praised and said to gain extra merit by the extension of their ordinary domestic chores to support the physical environment of the professional members, whether such chores be those of the Christian laywoman who cleans the church and arranges the flowers for the important festivals or those of the Buddhist village woman who prepares and delivers the morning and midday meals to the monks in their community (the *sangha*).

The ideology of some religious groups maintains that all members are equal and that all are equally expert or nonexpert in religious matters. Although women in these groups are equal members theoretically, often they are not so in reality, or there may be some ambivalence about their position. In early Gnostic

groups, which existed in the first centuries CE and are often regarded as among the first heretical groups within Christianity, all
members could equally access salvation through their spiritual insight or knowledge (*gnosis*). Thus, women were able to be counted
among the professionals and office bearers in many of these
groups. However, the theology of some Gnostic groups included
negative doctrine regarding "femaleness," which referred to the
ability to bear children. Such activity was seen as negative since
by bringing more people into the world, women were ensuring
that the spiritual heavenly light, which the Gnostics believed was
trapped in human beings and other living things in the evil material world, would be further trapped in the new generations.
Because of this potential for negative activity associated with a
woman's sexual function, some Gnostic texts call for women to
become male in order to gain salvation. I return to this point in
chapter 3.

THE FEMALE ADEPT/THE EXCEPTIONAL WOMAN/THE RELIGIOUS PRO-
FESSIONAL. In groups that draw a clear distinction between professional and nonprofessional members, the lines of separation
may be drawn on the basis of perceptions of spiritual giftedness
or on qualities such as intellectual ability, nobility, or class. There
are a variety of roles I could mention here apart from perhaps
the most obvious role of nun, which can be found in both Western and Eastern traditions. In books that detail the functions of
women religious professionals, you will find experts such as tantric
masters, Zen masters, Buddhist adepts, female saints, female
shamans, nuns, Christian priests, and Jewish rabbis.

The Buddhist and Confucian traditions, and the Christian tradition to some extent, number many princesses and queens both
as adepts and as financial supporters and founders of monasteries. Medieval Christian tradition indicates that many noblewomen
were in charge of monasteries of nuns or of double monasteries
of nuns and monks.

THE WOMAN WITH STATUS, NOT NECESSARILY AN ADEPT OR RELIGIOUS
PROFESSIONAL. Women may belong to the expert group or to the
religious professionals simply by the fact that they belong to, or

are connected to, an elite or powerful class either within the religious group or in society generally. There are many occasions where wives or mothers or daughters of holy men or male religious professionals come to some prominence. Many books on Islam and women, for example, use Muhammad's wives, especially Aisha, as useful models for modern Muslim women wishing to improve their status.[6]

Some female figures who have some status within the early years of a tradition may very well gain more status as the tradition continues. Thus, the position of the Virgin Mary has gained more and more status within some denominations of Christianity over the centuries. Even in the Christian gospels of the New Testament, there is clearly an increase in status over time—from the earliest gospel, the Gospel of Mark, in which Mary is depicted as part of the family of Jesus, which is held in low regard because of their treatment of him, to the later Gospel of Luke, where she is already in the preliminary stages of becoming the virgin mother of an incarnate god.

In her book *Mythological Woman*, Denise Lardner Carmody tells an interesting story regarding the status of Muhammad's daughter Fatimah in contemporary Iran. She relates that in January 1989, there was an interview on Teheran Radio in which a woman said she could not accept Muhammad's daughter as a role model. The broadcast director was sentenced to five years in jail, the three directors of Teheran Radio's ideology group were sentenced to four years each, and all received fifty lashes. The Ayatollah announced that if the insult had been deliberate, the person responsible would have been executed.[7] The story surely indicates, even in some perverse way, the status given to Muhammad's daughter within Islam.

Women's Choice for Religion: The Religious Identity of Women in Religious Groups

As with all human beings, at different times of a woman's life she has the capacity or predisposition to be interested in religion to a greater or lesser extent and for different purposes. Sometimes she may want a more meditative solitary experience, sometimes an experience of physical community. Women with small children may choose a religious group that caters to young children, whether in the practical sense of child care or in the more spiritual sense of its theology. Even where there is relatively egalitarian housekeeping and child rearing, evidence suggests that the woman takes primary responsibility for these tasks and will therefore be more likely to juggle her religious choices to fit her domestic responsibilities.

Certain cultural or political situations make participation in religion a requirement. Treating it as optional is either literally not thinkable or is so dangerous and life threatening that a choice against it cannot be reasonably considered. For much of human history, a personal "choice" about the faith map one used would have been inconceivable. Less frequently, alternative faith maps would have been available, but choosing a map other than the official one could have brought suffering and sometimes death.

When I spoke above of natural religious communities, it became clear that a separate religious identity does not exist for members of these communities, so choice about religion is literally not thinkable. This does not mean, however, that it is impossible to choose among ways of expressing religiosity even in small ways within such groups. The question of a clearly differentiated religious membership may seem an easier one for women within universalizing religions, but there may be, in actual fact, just as many constraints against women believers identifying themselves differently in this situation as against those in natural religious communities, depending on their circumstances within family and cultural groups and the cohesiveness of these groups.

In cultures where women are limited socially in some ways—in dress, in physical access to the world at large, in intellectual or spiritual access to the teachings and rituals of their religion, in elementary education—there may be a further decrease in women's possibilities of choice relative to men's possibilities.

Today, as a result of women's movements, many women are making a choice for the first time about remaining in their traditional religion or not, perhaps even choosing to move to what might be considered by their social group as a nontraditional or less acceptable religion. A choice against religion, if not made from indifference, can still imply a relationship to religion. People may choose against a religious identity and in that denial may be actively engaged against specific religious groups. A stance against organized religion does not preclude a person's self-identification as religious or her engagement with a sacred power or extraordinary reality.

LANGUAGE ABOUT WOMEN AND RELIGION

In the first hermeneutical exercise in chapter 1, I suggested questions for personal reflection such as the following:

- What race am I?
- What is my gender?
- What is my culture?
- Where do I stand socially within my culture?

These seem relatively straightforward questions, and constitute the first level for contextualizing yourself in the interpretive process. I need to probe more deeply now to pick up the two terms that delineate the parameters of this study. I propose the following questions for you as a "listener" and as one attempting to be open to finding new questions as you engage in the conversation with the material.

- Who am I in relation to the term *woman* as I listen to these women?
- Do I see how I relate to the term *woman* as relevant to what I am listening to/reading and interpreting?
- How do I allow my mind to be broad enough to hear all of the possibilities for the women who tell their stories and to have other understandings of the term *woman*?
- Who am I in relation to the term *religion* as I listen to these women?
- How do I allow my mind to be broad enough to hear all the women speak about their religious experiences and to have other understandings of the term *religion*?

I would argue that the perception of what a woman is provides a basic key for understanding both how women speak about their own experiences and how religious groups describe the religious life of women.[8]

The Question of the Identity or "Self" of a Woman

The question "What is a woman?" is not a simple one, as I have outlined briefly in the introduction. Probing more deeply, how can I answer that question, for example, within the Buddhist tradition with its concepts about the illusory nature of the human self and the quest for liberation from this illusion that I am a "self" in order to experience "no-self"? Religious traditions may differ quite markedly in the views they hold of human identity or the possibility of a human "self," and this can make our study of women's religious experience more complex than it might first appear to be.

In this section, I need to say a few words briefly about the variety of ideas concerning identity within different cultures and within different religious traditions so that you can keep these ideas in mind in the following chapters.

Reflection on what a human identity is has always interested thinkers in the East and West and has been one of the key questions that religious traditions address. Who am I? What is the purpose of my life? What is my origin, and what is my destiny? How am I different from the animals? Some cultures frame these questions collectively but always in a specific context of person, place, and time.

One of the most influential ways in which theories about self and identity are currently constructed in Western discourse began with modern Western psychoanalytical theory. Two of the earliest scholars involved in psychoanalysis, Sigmund Freud and Carl Jung, focused on the individual to generate theories about personality and used the key term *ego* ("I") in conjunction with other terms to represent the complexity of human personality.

For Freud, the human person comprises three main aspects: at the top, so to speak, is the *superego* ("the above-I"), which is the aspect of personality formed by all the influences, expectations, and attitudes of the outer world (family, society, etc.); at the base is the *id* ("it"), which is unconscious and unaware of itself, in which one finds all the basic physical drives, especially those dealing with hunger and survival (to eat, kill, engage in sex); in the middle, and trying to satisfy the demands of both superego and id, is the *ego* ("I"), the aspect of a human being that makes the choice for certain behaviors, influenced by both superego and id.

As this model has filtered down into everyday popular usage, many people use terms like ego quite easily or perhaps know enough to talk about an "Oedipal complex" or a "Freudian slip." So pervasive have these ideas become in Western culture that it is easy to mistake them for a description of reality rather than see them as constituting one metaphor alongside others for understanding the human being in her or his world. As with any other theory, it is necessary to understand this theory in the political and cultural context in which it arose and in particular to understand what presuppositions have been made about human beings and especially about women where the theory is applied to them.

Women have not been slow to critique psychoanalytical theories as part of the feminist enterprise in the West, and rightly so. Freud proposed that women have weakly developed superegos, a state that is also related to the "penis envy" that he claims girls and women experience. This reminds me of the ancient philosophical description of women as misbegotten males, which has underpinned so much of Western Christian theological development. If the founders of modern psychoanalytical theory base their theories in relation to women on a presupposition that women begin from a position of inferiority or lack, whether that refers to their biological sexual development (lack of a penis) or their development of a sense of self (lack of a well socialized and supported ego), then I must be careful of these presuppositions as they support and are taken on by societies (including religious groups within those societies), perhaps in an unreflected way. And if women have been disadvantaged in many societies by the kinds of preferential and supportive treatment given to boys and men, such that women's egos are not strong, then I must be careful to differentiate between disadvantage by the structures of society and disadvantage through an inherent psychological/physical lack.[9]

Western psychological theories are just one element of influence on Western (and to some extent Eastern) culture and its view of the identity of women. Of course, both Western and Eastern philosophies have a much longer history of reflection on the "self" than modern psychoanalytical theory. Some philosophers have worked very specifically within religious traditions to propose views of the self. Within these traditions, much of the reflection is based on some feeling or observation or idea about the unsatisfactory quality of the life of human beings—whether that is described in terms of sinfulness, selfishness, a lack of spiritual power, suffering, impermanence, human mortality, or the inability of humans to hold onto transitory extraordinary experiences like love, grief, or ecstasy. Some of this unsatisfactoriness is found in the individual or the community or simply in "the world." Its cause may be found within individuals (they are spiritually asleep, they are ignorant, they are weak, they have forgotten some first pure state, they have fallen into sin, etc.) or within some external power such as demons or a power of evil.

Practices or devotions by which believers come to terms with this state of affairs of unsatisfactoriness are usually focused on setting right the inner consciousness/soul/life-principle of the individual or on setting right something within the community or world at large, and religious traditions may be more focused on the identity of the individual or on the communal identity in their wisdom about how this should be done. Over time, too, certain traditions may tend more toward one aspect than the other. Indeed, certain traditions may even hold conflicting philosophical views on identity concurrently. This is easily illustrated within Hinduism.

Hinduism uses the term *bhakti* to describe a personal or communal response arising from a felt connection with sacred power or a specific deity. This response may be made in public forms of worship as well as in private ritual. While this is a widespread idea and religious path within Hinduism, the understanding of how the personal relationship between devotee and deity reaches fruition may differ from one philosophical school to another, generally in relation to concepts about the way in which a human self (*atman*) is either dissolved into, or remains separate from, the universal Self (*Brahman*) with which it strives to be in relationship, and which is represented by a particular deity. Within the Śaṃkara school, the relationship between the human self and the universal Self relies on the human self remaining intact. Within the Rāmānuja school, on the other hand, a separate human identity is rejected, and the relationship with the universal Self leads to the human self being dissolved or annihilated, or the self integrated into Self.

In contrast to Hinduism, Buddhism presents a particularly interesting dilemma, since Buddhists deny the very idea of a self or Self that is unchangeable and imperishable. For Buddhists, each human being is simply a composition of five related aspects known as "groups of grasping" (*upadanakhandhas*)—material form, feeling, cognition, the ability to initiate action or shape character, discriminative consciousness—that are all characterized as unsatisfactory, impermanent, the cause of suffering. But these very aspects cause human beings to think of themselves as having an identity, an "I," and thus as something that has permanence. Buddhist practice is concerned with the purification of these aspects of a person with a view to showing the person or waking up the person (*nirvana*) to how these aspects are impermanent and to the reality that there is no unitary self—there is only not-Self. Thus, suffering or its cause (i.e., grasping) is undermined because there is nothing, no self, that can be grasped. This contrasts with the spiritual quest of Hinduism in the Buddha's day of trying to find and liberate the true Self in a person.[10]

In comparison with Hinduism and Buddhism, Judaism, Christianity, and Islam are much more uniform. These are groups that predicate a God with an "I," and their fundamental system of organization and moral law is essentially social. Kinship with one another and kinship or friendship with deity is the basis of each system. The human self is basically social, such that people belong in communities—Jewish synagogue community, Christian church/community (*ekklesia*), Islamic community (*ummah*)—so the "self" of the community, the people as a whole, is of more importance than the individual "self." Even more basic, within Christianity, reality finds its foundation in the trinity of persons in the Christian god, and this collective relating unity forms the basis of all relating within the Christian community.

What binds the concepts about collective identity together is the idea of persons as relating. Some ancient and contemporary spiritualities also emphasize the indivisibility of individual identity from the life of community, though that community may be viewed as including all sentient beings or the entire planet, including what has previously been thought of as inanimate material. Here, the concern is less for the unique value of the individual being than for "the health of biotic communities."[11] When speaking of this concept, Rosemary Radford Ruether takes the idea from the Book of Genesis in the Jewish scriptures that humans are made in the "image of God" and the care of nature is given into their hands. She draws the ethical meaning from this that not only should human beings not destroy nature but they, in fact, have "a much more comprehensive responsibility for the preservation of nature."[12]

When I consider the view of human beings within the traditional religions and within spiritualities that focus on individual identity within the web of relationships of the living, breathing, and constantly renewing planet, I must be careful not to think of identity as a fixed category. If identity is shaped by interactions with others and the world around us, then it cannot be appropriate to see identity as something fixed but rather as a process, and religious groups that focus on processes of conversion for membership implicitly teach this. As George Coe remarks, "Conversion is a step in the creation of a self—the actual coming to be of a self."[13]

In the ordinary run of religious groups, whether they are coterminous with a cultural group or not, there are rituals to do with identity where children assume the identity of the group and become members in a formal sense—Jewish circumcision, infant Christian baptism, Hindu twice-born ritual. This process of becoming a member is not seen by the group as conversion but as a growth in faith or growth toward another level of belonging, so even for these groups identity is not fixed.

How does this discussion of identity relate to women's religious experience? Social and religious groups have profound influence on each other, as I have suggested earlier in this chapter. The assigning of religious identity to women most often works from the basic identity assigned by society. I will come back to this point in the next chapter, but I will give an example here to make the point clear.

In the Buddhist spirit cults in northeast Thailand, the chief mediums (those who "channel" spirits or communicate for others with spirits) tend to be male, but subordinate mediums are most often female. This is the only sphere in which females have a dominant ritual role to play, and that role is based on a social view about the kind of temperament that a woman typically has. Villagers believe that: "Women are by temperament prone to possession and the spirits possess them because they are soft and penetrable; therefore they are effective hosts. . . ."[14] The view about women's temperament has further implications than the assigning of the role. Because women are soft and penetrable (note the possible sexual connotation), they are also more likely to be possessed by evil spirits and to become sick, and thus, women are also more likely than men to need exorcisms. Those women who become mediums are not necessarily thought to be powerful people. Generally, the mediums themselves have previously suffered illness or fits or states of dislocation because of the spirits, and they have only been cured when they agree to be the mediums for the spirits.

The influence also works in reverse. Religious systems in their turn have influence upon social views. Very often within religious traditions, religious teaching is used to justify a certain social and religious role for women in a system preordained by some transcendent authority mediated by certain powerful men or religious professionals. On occasion, social and religious views will come into conflict. In her introduction to European medieval women writers, Wilson points out that the medieval Christian model situated consecrated virgins first (i.e., women who had taken vows within the Church to remain virgins), then widows, and lastly married women. The medieval social model, however, placed the married women first (in the hope of producing the highest good—a male heir), followed by widows and then spinsters.[15] I would propose that the conflict implicit in these two models was resolved by the Christian medieval emphasis on veneration of Mary, the Virgin Mother, who incorporates the two prime categories of the virgin and the mother within her single figure.

Religion Defining Women

When listening to the stories about women's religious experience, you may hear different, perhaps even contradictory, voices. In my example of the hermeneutical process in chapter 1, I showed how Catholic papal statements about women in relationship to a creator God were based upon a view of women summed up in the key physical symbol of the womb. You may also have heard my own voice speaking in a very different way within that example.

The religious institutional answers to the question, "What is a woman?," are often focused on the biological and social functions of women within the private domestic sphere, which have a long tradition in Eastern and Western cultures. The example I have just used of medieval European Christianity and medieval European society categorizes women according to their potential for marriage or their marital status. Many religions concern themselves intimately with the biological and social life stages of women. Thus, in many religious groups there is an insistence on virginity for unmarried women; there are rules governing the role of the menstrual or menopausal woman; there are taboos surrounding either menstruation or childbirth and its aftermath; there are psychological or physical penalties for the childless woman; there are rules concerning women's marriage or access to divorce or their experience of widowhood. I will return to this point in much more detail in the next chapter.

As a religious group searches for an answer concerning the nature of women, it allocates particular roles suitable for women and defines other roles that are unsuitable. The giving of roles in turn supports and strengthens the definitions. As soon as the features of a certain group are defined or in process of definition, boundaries are set with regard to thinking, the cycle of thought tends to be closed off, and breakthrough cannot occur without breaking the whole theological or ideological pattern. On the one hand, this may be seen as a limiting process; on the other hand, there may be opportunities available for women within the structures that do not exist outside them.

The feminist movements in this century, especially, have begun to have some effect on a process of redefinition in many religious groups, as Rita Gross has comprehensively outlined[16]—although no one would deny that this is only a small beginning. On the simplest level, feminist criticism understands religion to be one of the key players in the oppressive sociopolitical structures of patriarchy. At the beginning of the current wave of feminist movements in the West, especially, the criticism against religion was so strong that many gatherings of feminists would not allow religious topics for discussion, especially when raised by women still actively working for change as continuing members of religious groups. It was felt also that a focus on the spiritual would prevent people from taking political action. I wonder if such a view of religion still operates in some quarters, especially when a recent book on contemporary Australian feminism provides no treatment whatsoever of any religious subject matter.[17]

Women Defining "Spirituality" and "Religion"

Clearly, feminist scholars have made a tremendous contribution in the recent past to the redefinition of concepts like "religion" and "spirituality," either in studies explicitly devoted to that purpose or within general theologies. However, ordinary women within traditions have also given great impetus to the reinterpretation of these concepts. Stories from women about their religious experiences, both within and outside of established religious groups, provide a variety of concepts related to a sacred power or extraordinary reality. One of the intriguing features of the contemporary stories of women is not so much that there is such variety in the language and symbols used in the telling but that these stories are of interest to women from very different backgrounds. The breadth of the dialogue in women's spirituality at the moment is too great for one to gain an overview, but it is possible to get some idea of it in small contexts. Over the last fifteen years or so, I have been a participant in a number of women's groups interested in some way in religion or theology or spirituality that seem to "slip" easily between the concepts and rituals of institutionalized religion and noninstitutionalized religion. It is not unusual, for example, to have practitioners of Wicca involved in dialogue with Catholic nuns over a range of spiritual issues.

In chapter 1, I noted that religious groups may mediate, but do not wholly encompass, the experience of sacred power, which is their focus. If you have been reading any contemporary women's stories about religious experience, you may have noticed that many women seem to prefer to speak of experiences of sacred power in terms of spirituality rather than religion. Most often, the writers appear to be speaking of "religion" as synonymous with "religions." They imply that *spirituality* is a broader term than *religion*, and that it encompasses all experience of the sacred in a way that "religion" cannot. In fact, some writers may not see a link at all between spirituality and institutional religion. They express and practice their spirituality not in the rituals of institutional religion but in ways such as political and environmental activism. However, both traditional institutional religion and movements of feminist spirituality contend that the inner personal experience of the sacred is not enough—the experience demands and is not complete without expression in either the traditional forms of ritual, prayer, or good works or in sociopolitical activity.

Ursula King's description of spirituality as something that permeates all human endeavor, "an age-old human quest to seek fulfilment, liberation and pointers towards transcendence amidst the welter of human experience,"[18] gives some idea of the breadth of understanding of this term within women's spiritual writing.

King's definition seems to be close to the understanding of religion that I put forward for natural religious communities earlier in this chapter.

Because feminist spiritualities do not tend to draw on the traditional forms of institutional religion for dogmatic expression, you may not find these reflections always or even generally in the usual places one looks for theological works. New spiritual spaces are opening up increasingly in women's imaginative work in fiction and film as a source for religious knowledge and reflection.

Because of the disagreements about how a spirituality based on personal relationship to sacred power is to be understood in relation to religion, perhaps it might be helpful to look for a new description. One possible term might be *devotion* or *bhakti*, a term I have used previously in this chapter when discussing ideas about the self/Self in Hinduism. Devotion may involve public forms of worship as well as private ritual but essentially arises from a felt connection with the sacred power and finds its expression in a personal response in the individual or community. Thus, some people may be devotional without being intentional members of a religious group; members of religious groups may be devotional within the context of a particular religion.

The difficulty with using a term like devotion or bhakti is that not all traditions or individuals follow such a spiritual path. Thus, Buddhists aim for a loss of ego rather than the development or maintenance of ego in an "I-Thou" type relation to a deity or sacred power. Some forms of yoga as a spiritual path within Hinduism are concerned with duty (*karma-yoga*) or knowledge (*jnana-yoga*) rather than with any felt personal connection with deity.

One of the key movements in the recent past within Western feminist spirituality centers on what has become known as neopaganism; that is, the exploration and recreation or reimagining of old, pre-Christian European or non-European traditions. This is not a movement that is in any way homogeneous: Some groups are interested in the Goddess, under a variety of guises or identities; others are interested in various traditions of shamanism; others in witchcraft, and so on. Generally, one could describe the core belief of these various groups as earth-based spirituality, as Starhawk explains in relation to her spirituality: "Goddess is embodied in the living world, in the human, animal, plant, and mineral communities and their interrelationships."[19]

The link with earth-based spirituality is particularly apt for those groups that honor the Goddess, since many goddesses were key agents in the cycles of the regeneration and growth of crops and of human families. One of the important themes of the agricultural myths from many ancient cultures is the dying and rising/revivification of a male god. The focus in the analysis of these myths has been most often on this god, and yet, the focal figure is really the female goddess, who is the savior or lifegiver to the dead god. The death of the male figure dramatizes the way or the mystery by which the seed must die in the earth before creation can begin. The female figure represents the earth, which revives the seed. However, the Goddess who is spoken of in many of these groups is not any one goddess from the variety of mythologies available but rather a universal figure much like the concept of an earth-mother goddess that many maintain was the first expression of the sacred power in anthropomorphic form in prehistoric communities. I will return to a discussion of Goddess religions/spiritualities in both chapters 4 and 5.

CONCLUSION

In this chapter, I have painted in very broad strokes some of the women-in-religion issues ranging from the definitions of women by religions and the way in which women have reacted toward these to the way in which women are members of religious groups and their ability to choose to be members or not. Finally, I have looked at the way in which women may describe themselves as religious or spiritual without their belonging to a formally established religious group. In the next chapter, I look in detail at the implications of how religions define women and the assigning of women's place to the margins of traditions.

NOTES

1. See Victoria Bernal, "Gender, Culture, and Capitalism: Women and the Remaking of Islamic 'Tradition' in a Sudanese Village," *Comparative Studies in Society and History*, vol. 36 (1994), pp. 36–67.

2. Karma Lekshe Tsomo, ed., *Sakyadhita: Daughters of the Buddha* (Ithaca, N.Y.: Snow Lion Publications, 1988), pp. 26–27; Tsomo characterizes such action as "intimidation."

3. Alex Owen, *The Darkened Room: Women, Power, and Spiritualism in Late Nineteenth Century England* (London: Virago, 1989), p. 153.

4. Owen, *Darkened Room*, pp. 168–201.

5. Gwendolyn Bryant, "The French Heretic Beguine: Marguerite Porete," in Katharina M. Wilson, ed., *Medieval Women Writers* (Athens, Ga.: University of Georgia Press, 1984), pp. 207–9.

6. See, e.g., the second section in Barbara Freyer Stowasser, *Women in the Qur'an, Traditions, and Interpretation* (New York: Oxford University Press, 1994).

7. Denise Lardner Carmody, *Mythological Woman: Contemporary Reflections on Ancient Religious Stories* (New York: Crossroad, 1992), p. 114.

8. Maura O'Neill makes a similar argument that philosophical discussion of key terms like *person, ultimate reality, knowledge,* and *experience* is crucial for interreligious dialogue; see especially her first chapter, "The Nature of the Human Person," in *Women Speaking, Women Listening: Women in Interreligious Dialogue* (Maryknoll, N.Y.: Orbis Books, 1990), pp. 3–12.

9. As Elizabeth Mayer points out, even if the experience of penis envy can be substantiated and observed clinically, such feelings of envy or inferiority on a woman's/girl's part do not necessarily lead to actual inferiority to men "in terms of a woman's sense of justice, intellectual curiosity, capacity to implement her ideas independent of a man's approval, and so forth. . . . Learning how to deal, in productive ways, with feelings of envy or of insecurity or of being different from other people is, after all, central to the challenge of growing up for any individual, male or female," Elizabeth Lloyd Mayer, "Appendix: An Appraisal of the Psychology of Women in Personality Theories: Freud, Reich, Adler, and Jung," in James Fadiman and Robert Frager, eds., *Personality and Personal Growth* (New York: Harper & Row, 1976), pp. 465–66.

10. Peter Harvey, "Buddhism," in Jean Holm and John Bowker, eds., *Human Nature and Destiny* (London: Pinter Publishers, 1994), pp. 21–23.

11. Rosemary Radford Ruether, *Gaia and God: An Ecofeminist Theology of Earth Healing* (New York: HarperSan Francisco, 1992), p. 221.

12. Ruether, *Gaia and God*, p. 222.

13. George Albert Coe, *The Psychology of Religion* (Chicago: University of Chicago Press, 1916), p. 171.

14. S. J. Tambiah, *Buddhism and the Spirit Cults of North-east Thailand* (Cambridge: Cambridge University Press, 1970), p. 283.

15. Katharina M. Wilson, ed., *Medieval Women Writers* (Athens: University of Georgia Press, 1984), p. x.

16. Rita M. Gross, *Feminism and Religion: An Introduction* (Boston: Beacon Press, 1996).

17. Kate Pritchard Hughes, ed., *Contemporary Australian Feminism* (Melbourne: Longman Cheshire, 1994).

18. Ursula King, *Women and Spirituality: Voices of Protest and Promise* (Women in Society, London: Macmillan Education, 1989), p. 5.

19. Starhawk, "Feminist, Earth-based Spirituality and Ecofeminism," in Judith Plant, ed., *Healing the Wounds: The Promise of Ecofeminism* (Philadelphia: New Society Publishers, 1989), p. 177.

3

Voices from Offstage — Marginal Experience, Marginal Language

—ᴍ—

In the second chapter, I spoke of religion and women, and of women's religious experience. In chapters 3 and 4, I will discuss women's religious experience in more detail, first as marginal experience and second as central experience. Let me first situate the discussion once again in relation to the hermeneutical model of three elements in chapter 1—phenomenon, method of study, and the one studying. I will concentrate here on the phenomenon of women's religious experience and go into a little more detail.

The Experience and the Relating of The Experience

The material that I study—the phenomenon—is related to the religious experience of women in some way. It may be that I am studying the experience itself, or I may be dealing with materials that I mentioned in chapter 1 that are associated with that experience (written or spoken words, rituals, authoritative statements,

dance, song, painting, drama, paraphernalia [e.g., dress, uten-
sils], architecture). There are a variety of ways in which the experience or the material might be available to me for study.

p – religious experience
h
e
n
o – primary text/firsthand description/reflection
m
e
n
o – secondary text/secondhand description/reflection
n

First, I might see someone have a religious experience at first
hand. I may see/hear/touch a woman involved in religious activity of some kind, whether it be an individual experience or a
communal experience in which she is participating. Second, I
might listen to women speak about their experience in the first
person, whether they speak or write or sculpt or sing or mime
and so on. Third, I can listen to others speak of women's experience in the third person, describing it or interpreting it.

As I said in chapter 1, I cannot talk about this process without
also reflecting on what I am doing as the one who listens, without reflecting on which method I am using to help me listen, both
to those who speak in the first person about their own experience
and to those who describe what others have experienced.

It might seem that being a participant observer of a woman's
religious experience makes the study easier or better than listening to or reading secondhand material. However, when I watch
or listen as a participant oberver, I still remain a step away from
the woman's experience, because I only see the way in which the
woman expresses the experience that she is having; I do not have
her explanation or description of her experience. I am left to rely
on my own interpretation of the meaning of the experience, and
my ideas might be quite different from what the person herself
thinks. So, I do not want to get caught up here in questions about

what is better or truer in the various levels of material that I might access, although I myself may well feel better about being closer to the expression than reading about it. On the other hand, I am wary of those who might say that secondhand accounts are better for study, because I cannot take for granted that the woman herself understands what is happening to her. While this might be a true statement, I am suspicious of any proposal to take away a woman's authority to speak of her own experience, particularly since the silence of women's voices is at the core of this current study.

Women's religious experience has been generally described, categorized, and interpreted by male religious professionals within religious traditions. It is clear that this fact alone has implications for the potential marginalization of women's experience, and that if this occurs, there are some difficult questions to face: How can I listen to, or even hear, the voices of women on the margin? How do I speak with women on the margin? What language do I need? What language is being used by the women who speak to me? What language is used by others to tell me about the experience of women on the margin? If I am a woman myself, what is my language? Do I have a better chance of listening and hearing if I am a woman?

The questions that relate to the kind of language being used in the sources available for study are very important. I might think that if I could find firsthand sources from women about their experience, I would have less difficulty than if I were to try to study their experience through a layer of marginalizing language in secondhand accounts. But I have to ask: In firsthand accounts of their religious experience, what language/symbols do women have to speak about their experience? Do they have a language of their own? If not, whose will they borrow?

This is more than the problem all people face about a language that can express more or less satisfactorily a personal experience. Of course people struggle with language, religious or otherwise, to describe their own particular experiences. But the problem for women can be more than that—first, when religious language does not recognize them as people who have valid or important religious experiences; and second, when the religious language available to them may not fit their own gendered experience because male experience is considered the norm.

When I come to study firsthand or secondhand accounts of women's religious experience, I must ask, too, about the context of the language that is being used. This is a little like the attempt to contextualize the accounts according to the ideas about women's identity that I outlined in chapter 2. As with ideas about identity, language about women will change according to time and space. More explicitly, what are the social and political and religious issues at a particular time that influence the language of the accounts that I am reading?

Let me give just one example to make this clear. In reading the texts of the Christian New Testament and those passages in which women's experience is described, it is necessary to know that the society in which the texts arose and first functioned was a premodern society, organized on strict hierarchical lines from Roman emperor down to slave—and that the language of the text is the language of such a society. Within the New Testament writings, Sheila Briggs has analyzed passages from the letters of Paul and later letters said to be from Paul (sometimes called the Deutero-Pauline letters) in relation to this social setting, to see what might be the implications of the image she sees presented there of God as a "heavenly slaveowner."[1] She proposes that the letters use this heavily hierarchical language even when talking about the relation of a man and woman in marriage, so that there are passages where a wife is commanded to be submissive to her husband in everything. Thus a husband mirrors for his wife the relation that exists between God and human beings. Briggs sums up:

> The "love patriarchalism" (as biblical scholars refer to the rules of conduct for wives and husbands in Ephesians and Colossians) is part of a pattern of domination, which rests upon the dishonouring of Christians as part of their enslavement within the body of Christ.[2]

Finally, I should also ask what the motivations are of those who speak both at first hand and second hand about women's religious experience. It may be that the material I study was not meant to be available to any person other than the one who had the religious experience. In this case, I may be rather like an eavesdropper and I need to ask myself about the ethics of what I am doing. In firsthand or secondhand accounts that are intended to be heard or read by others, a number of motivations may be operating: Someone may wish to communicate what the experience was like in order to impress others, to give information about it, to convince others about it, to draw others to the same experience, or to share distress or elation or some other feeling about the experience. In describing the experience, a person may be trying to recapture the experience or the feelings associated with it, may be attempting to make sense of the experience, or may be wanting to discredit the experience of another. Of course, the motivations of the one who is describing the experience may not be explicit, but I may be able to pick up clues about the motivation from the kind of language and images used.

THE AUTHORITY OF RELIGIOUS AND ACADEMIC TRADITIONS

In this section and the following section, I am going to look more carefully at the lines of relationship between those who speak and those who listen or those who are silenced, as well as those who tell others how to speak and how to listen within the institutional perspective of religion. This discussion needs to take place with the acknowledgment that speaking and listening are founded on a usually nonarticulated sense or awareness of who I am as I speak or listen. Part of the analysis of how power operates in the speaking and listening process lies in exposing the connections between identity, authority, and the ability to speak or the requirement to listen.

In chapter 2, I wrote of how religious groups may assign identity to their members. In this section, I will discuss this process in much more depth with respect to the way that power operates in both religious groups and the academic arena and the way that

women and their religious experiences are marginalized as a result. When I attempt to listen to women's experiences, I must ask
not only what a religious tradition has to say about women's experience but also what the academic textbooks have to say about
that experience.

Those who have written, and still write, of religious experience
within the religious traditions are overwhelmingly male religious
professionals. Those who have written of religious experience within
the academic areas of theology or studies in religion also have been
overwhelmingly male, for the most part religious professionals
themselves or at least those who have had some theological training within a religious tradition. Both areas of influence—religious
traditions and the academic arena—are thoroughly imbued with a
language and world view that are normatively male.

Those academics who study religion in fields such as anthropology or sociology or history, and who are not from the ranks
of religious professionals, have gathered information in the past
generally only from male religious believers in order to gain
knowledge of religious experience. In some cases, it may not be
their intention to keep the women invisible. It may simply be that
the menfolk to whom the anthropologists speak do not know anything about the women's experience. It may also be that the
women are not free to speak of their experience to men, even for
the purposes of scholarship.[3]

Authority and orthodoxy are perceived by the academy in general as based above all in those who wield power, or are presumed
to wield power, within the hierarchical structures of the traditions,
such that religious experience is judged almost solely according
to the tenets and pronouncements of a small core of male religious professionals. As a result, the language used of women's experience is one in which men's experience is the norm, and
women's experience is often characterized as marginal, frighten-
ing, or dangerous or as superstition rather than real religion.

What suffers by such a clerical or text-based view of orthodoxy
in religious and academic communities is a more encompassing
picture of the breadth of the tradition and the experience of believers—male as well as female believers. However, female members may be more seriously disadvantaged.

Frédérique Marglin's work on the categories of auspiciousness and inauspiciousness as central to Hindu Tantra and bhakti traditions illustrates that these traditions are more open to women and female symbolism than is classical Brahmanism. However, the general Western view has been that Brahmanism constitutes the central and orthodox stream within Hinduism, rather than the bhakti or Tantra traditions, which are more popular or more esoteric and hence considered not quite so orthodox. Thus, Western students generally have a poorer understanding of the breadth of women's religious experience within Hinduism.[4]

Similarly, Leila Ahmed writes of the limitations on the view of women in Islam, and the limitations on Muslim women themselves, if one takes clerical text-based Islam as the only source of authority for the tradition. She claims that other sources from Sufi and Qarmati thought would provide liberation for women, such that Muslim women would not be compelled to make the intolerable choice between religious belief and their own autonomy and self-affirmation.[5]

There appears to be only meager interest in women's religious experience in academic textbooks, where one might expect to find comprehensive information. Sections in textbooks on Islam tell me little more than that Muslim women attend mosque perhaps only once a year or maybe not at all. Sections that deal with Christianity focus almost solely on a predominantly male clergy and its practices or its history. Textbooks tend to mention women as marginalized, as those not allowed to do such and such—or they are not mentioned at all.

The established religions have their own particular view of themselves. The history of textbook writing and academic writing on the traditions tends to follow that same line. I would suggest that the official documents of both religions and the academy offer a very limited view of membership, such that women's religious experience is by and large invisible in religious texts, academic texts, and lecture/seminar content concerned with religion—"real" religion. Even where women's experience has become acknowledged in academic circles, it continues to be labeled as marginal—and therefore of limited interest.

At this stage, I find myself asking with my students: Who de-

cides what constitutes the "fringe"? Who decides what "real" religion is? Do women's voices count at all? Who decides the kind of
Buddhism or Hinduism or Islam or Christianity or Judaism that
is to be taught? Do these religions as described in the textbooks
actually exist?

Why is women's religious experience still something mostly
"marginal" and optional to academic study (and often one of the
first subjects to be sacrificed when economic difficulties arise for
departments)? Why do so many women now prefer to talk about
their "spirituality" rather than their "religion"—as if, not having
been allowed previously to claim the word or the experience, they
want no part of it now?

MARGINALIZATION STRATEGIES
BY RELIGIOUS TRADITIONS

The Marginalization of Women in Religious Texts

At the beginning of this chapter, I suggested that there were implications for the marginalization of women's religious experience where religious experience in general has been described,
categorized, and interpreted by male religious professionals. In
literate cultures, where male professional scholars maintain religious tradition through the control of texts by writing them, interpreting them, or using them in ritual, women tend to be excluded both within and by means of those texts. Even where some
women in a tradition have had literacy skills, they have not been
permitted to be involved in the production and interpretation of
texts—and sometimes not even permitted to read the sacred texts.
As Andrew Kadel states, "Literacy is one thing; preparation to
teach and write theology, philosophy, or literature is something
else again."[6]

Women most often appear in religious texts when they are
problematical figures, immoral characters, the victims of men's
violence, or silent characters. To have even the merest glimpse of
the imbalance in the representation of female and male charac-

ters, one need only note in any typical religious text the number of times a woman is heard to speak in comparison with male characters. Of course, there are times when a powerful woman speaks with great effect—but I suggest that this is exceptional rather than normative.

Apart from spouses/mothers/daughters of great men, a few women are mentioned positively in texts when they are personally exceptional, larger than life. Even where a woman has been exceptional without having found a place in the religious hierarchy, the religious tradition will eventually give credit only in its own time-honored fashion and limited language.[7]

However, even when women's experience is mentioned, the mention may have very little to do with an actual perception about women and far more to do with clarifying a perception about men. Women are often only mentioned to highlight a certain male character in the text or to bring some aspect of men's experience more sharply into focus. Hilde Hein's study of spirituality within the Western tradition suggests that men's statements about women's spirituality (or lack of it) are not based on men's perceptions of women or a wish to define women's spirituality but, rather, are used to highlight men's self-perceptions.[8]

I must be careful in my analysis of the strategies of marginalization within religious texts. I would normally assume that where a woman appears in a text without being named, except as the wife or relative of some male, a strategy is at work that makes her marginal to the action or statement of the text. Yet Amina Wadud-Muhsin defends this practice in the Qur'an as a sign of respect in addressing women (though she does note that Mary, the mother of Jesus, is named).[9] I am willing to listen to Wadud-Muhsin's position as a Muslim woman on this text, but I would also want to investigate more thoroughly not only the concept about respect in not naming women but also a number of other things: the practice of referring to women only in relation to some male; the reason for the Qur'an actually naming Mary, the mother of Jesus; and other instances of the Qur'an referring to women in ways that would support the view that the text is concerned above all to respect women. I will return to this point in discussing criticisms of Western feminism and its analysis of structures of oppression of women in other cultures in chapter 5.

The Marginalization of Women in Religious Practice

Women's experience of being on the edge of religious practice should be seen as related to the marginalization of women in religious texts. The description and categorization of women in authoritative texts will often be used as a basis for excluding them from, or relegating them to the edge of, sacred space, ritual action, knowledge of texts or stories associated with ritual, and the role of the professional in the religious tradition.

WOMEN ON THE MARGIN WITHIN PROFESSIONAL HIERARCHICAL STRUCTURES. Women who have a role within the ranks of religious professionals may appear at first glance to have a place at the center of the tradition rather than on the margins, but the structures within traditions are such that even as professionals, women's situations may be quite ambivalent, always somehow less than men's positions, or with the trappings of status and power quite illusory. The acceptance of women into the ranks of the religious professionals may be no more than a cosmetic change. There may be no concurrent real change in attitude toward women either from the male religious professionals or from the general membership.

Women have been accepted into the ranks of Christian religious professionals in some denominations for some time now, but they are still more likely than not to be given jobs with a lower profile or less pay (when not entirely voluntary positions) in comparison with their male counterparts. Najah Manasra tells of the praise given to Palestinian women who died as martyrs during the Intifada, while since 1982 the social position of women has become more and more limited by the increasing influence of fundamentalist groups in Gaza.[10] Donald Swearer relates the story of the highly respected Buddhist teacher and nun Achan Runjuan, who was humiliated by monks because she was a woman.[11] Even in the Indian Tantric tradition, where women seem to have a dominant role—mirroring the female goddess Shakti, who is personified as the active principle in comparison with the male god Shiva, who is absolute stillness and passivity ("Shiva without Shakti is a corpse"[12])—Geoffrey Samuel suggests that women are often seen as mere accessories to the male partner.[13]

Of course, a central position given to women may be easily taken away if the real power at the center belongs to the male professionals. The General Assembly of the Presbyterian Church of Australia in September 1991 deleted Article 7 (by a vote of 115 for and 62 against), which had previously allowed for women's ordination on the same terms and conditions applicable to men.

Even where women have religious status there may be little recognition given to them in their general social context. I remember sitting on a ferry in Bangkok some years ago, watching Buddhist monks board for free while the Buddhist nuns who followed them were made to pay. This seems to me to be a case of nonrecognition. In other contexts there may be a degree of abuse, especially where women's actions appear to cut across socially acceptable behavior for women. Denise Carmody mentions the abuse that Chinese Buddhist nuns have had to endure because their celibate lifestyle contradicts the socially accepted Confucian view of family life as the highest good.[14] Steven Ozment mentions Protestant objections to, and closure of, Catholic convents during the Reformation, partly because the women within them were considered to be shirking their God-given responsibilities as women and Christians to marry and bear children.[15] Hindu female saints also have had to be strong in their devotion in the face of family continually throwing traditional female restrictions in their path.[16]

Because of the hierarchical system of power over others that is the means of ordering most religious traditions, women who are regarded positively or given some status within a tradition may themselves be caught up in that system. Women who are religious professionals may align themselves with their male colleagues to exclude in explicit or implicit ways other women in the tradition. There are stories of women in the traditions, too, where one woman with a position of status exercises power over another woman in just as oppressive a way as any man with similar status might do. The story of Sarah's abuse of Hagar in the Hebrew scriptures is a good example (Genesis 16 and 21).

In the Middle Ages in Europe, noble women often held the position of prioress or abbess in Christian monasteries. In a monastery, they inevitably made up the ranks of that group classified as "choir nuns." Beneath them in status were the lay nuns, who served the choir nuns by dealing with the world outside or with the lesser menial tasks of the monastery, leaving choir nuns free to pray. Abuse may not always result where female professionals have power over lay or lesser women members, but the structures certainly provide the incentive for those who wish to act in this way. Many women who have achieved a central position in traditions in the recent past (such as Zen masters, Vipassana teachers, Jewish rabbis, Christian priests and ministers) know well the danger of becoming central actors in such systems.

WOMEN ON THE MARGIN OUTSIDE OF PROFESSIONAL HIERARCHICAL STRUCTURES. All "lay" believers are marginal in relation to religious professionals if one is working from a perspective that sets religious professionals at the center of a tradition. The lower status of laypeople is sometimes acted out by their doing menial tasks for the religious professionals. Laywomen often work hard on behalf of religious professionals, for example, doing the domestic chores of cleaning sacred places or cooking for groups of monks or undertaking secretarial work for low pay or for no pay. Sometimes, though less frequently, laymen perform voluntary work for religious professionals.

However, there are clearly varying degrees of status between female and male lay believers. Laymen are often more highly visible in ritual or in a social sense than are laywomen—a Buddhist layman who finances the building of a temple and monastery complex for Buddhist monks is more visible and gains more merit than the Buddhist laywoman who brings the monks their midday meal; the Christian layman who sits on the parish council as the finance advisor, or the Christian layman who works outside in the grounds of the church, mowing the lawn or doing heavy physical work, is often more socially visible than the Christian laywoman who sweeps the church each week.

WOMEN ON THE EDGE OF, OR EXCLUDED FROM, CONSTRUCTED SACRED SPACE. Women's experience of the edge of sacred space is almost like a permanent liminal or threshold state—whether that is within structures for worship or out in open public spaces during religious festivals. Again, there are clearly varying degrees of status between female and male lay believers that are evident in the place given to women. Male and female lay believers may be separated in sacred places, with the men closer to the center of the ritual action. The sections for women are lower in status, on the edge or withdrawn on a balcony or behind a curtain. Laymen may be allowed to perform certain functions in ritual—may actually be allowed into the holiest spaces normally reserved for male religious professionals—that are closed to laywomen.

In extreme cases, women are not permitted or encouraged to enter constructed sacred spaces. In the late 1970s in North India, Shibani Roy found that out of a sample of three hundred women, not one had ever prayed in a mosque. In some special circumstances, old women had gone to a mosque to listen to lectures.[17]

WOMEN OUTSIDE CONSTRUCTED PUBLIC SACRED SPACE. Where women engage in public or private practices outside of the public sacred spaces controlled by male religious professionals, their activity is often labeled "just social" (i.e., not really religious), or is seen as superstitious or irreligious. Julie Marcus gives a good example of this situation when describing pilgrimages (ziyaret) by Muslim women to small village shrines and larger city shrines (the shrines are overwhelmingly visited by women), often considered "un-Islamic" by clerics.[18] She writes in particular of the shrine tomb of Susuz Dede in Izmir, where the rites appear to be very simple and thus are easily dismissed as primitive or superstitious by the clerics. Marcus remarks that such labeling is "crucial to maintaining a set of gender relations in which women are subordinate, and denies that women's rites are, in reality, deeply integrated within Turkish culture and Islam."[19]

I could also cite the early Christian saint Augustine, who objected to his mother's practice of setting out food at the grave sites of saints, calling it "very like the superstition of the Gentiles." He expressed approval that the Catholic bishop Ambrose had forced his mother, among others, to give up the practice.[20]

SOCIAL MARGINS = RELIGIOUS MARGINS. Generally speaking, religious traditions differentiate between men and women in religious terms by virtue of gender difference in much the same way as is done in the social context of the tradition. Most traditions give social status to women only in the domestic sphere, as social custom does, marriage and the home being the center of both their social and religious functions, though the home is much less important space in the eyes of the religious tradition than that constructed sacred space controlled and used by the religious professionals.

When I use the term *home* I am not implying the set space of a house or home in its entirety. Houses may consist of spaces that are private for one or more members of the family, or spaces for the entire family, or spaces that are accessible to the public. Homes and private and public spaces within them may be thought of differently in different cultures or historical periods. In her study of a second-century CE villa on Cyprus, Christine Kondoleon remarks: "Unlike the nineteenth-century bourgeois who withdrew from public life into his private drawing room, Romans commanded their domestic interiors as public stages integrating commercial, social, and familial practices."[21] Thus a woman may not count all parts of the house as accessible to her, or parts of the house may be denied to her at certain times. Leonard Swidler observed in Palestine during the 1970s that women were absent from meals and did not serve the meals when male guests were present, and this held for Arab, Christian, Druze, Jewish, and Muslim homes.[22]

The home is the "sacred space" for women, though women themselves might not judge it to be sacred. Sometimes it is clearly not sacred to those who initiate abuse of women in it. Thus, one should treat the word "status" with some caution. While there are degrees of reward for women for functions associated with the home, principally the bearing of sons, it is also clear from the statistics on domestic violence and the sexual abuse of women and children that women are also frequently marginalized even within the space that is meant to be their central space.

Abdur Doi's confessional statement about women in Islamic law is a good example of the synthesis of social and religious views about women:

> Allah has created man and woman to play distinct roles in human society and a woman's biology and physique best suit her, at base, for the maternal role so necessary in the creation of healthy and happy families. . . . Ignorance of these fundamental facts has led promoters of feminism to believe that both sexes should have the same responsibilities.[23]

Susan Wadley points to the same dichotomy of the sphere of influence of men and women within Hinduism, stating that women's rituals and their desires expressed in those rituals are focused on the home and the welfare of the family, while men are concerned primarily for the world outside the home.[24] This is supported by Julia Leslie's statement that, within Hinduism, women are not free to renounce the domestic context that identifies them, in order to take up an ascetic life as men may do.[25] Although Leslie's statement is generally true, there are instances of Hindu women becoming ascetics (*sādhvīs*).[26]

In Doi's statement, the authority of the deity is used to support social views and structures. Religious myths are particularly powerful in this regard, where social domestic views of women may be supported either by negative or positive views of women within the myths.

The negative view is taken, for example, in one of the Gnostic versions about how the Light fell from the heavenly region and became trapped in the flawed/evil material world. The myth, as told in the Gnostic text *The Hypostasis of the Archons* 2, 4–18, describes how one of the heavenly powers called Sophia (Wisdom) is overcome by desire for the high god, the heavenly Father. Desire is not a good thing because it makes a person irrational. Because Sophia is weakened by desire—a typical female thing—she is tricked by the evil powers, and she subsequently acts without her male heavenly partner, giving birth to a defective child, sometimes called an aborted fetus, the demiurge Ialdabaoth. He is the evil ignorant god responsible for the creation of the material world and for the entrapment of Light in its darkness. Such a story illustrates both the inherent weakness of women and the tragedy that occurs when women take initiative in their own right without their male partner.

The positive view is taken in Hindu myths about Sita, the wife of Ram (a manifestation of the great god Vishnu), which depict her as stillness as opposed to Ram's ceaseless activity. She is "passive, the object of males' desires, the victim of their tricks, the prize of their contests and wars. . . . She is a model of the orthodox Hindu construction of 'wife.' "[27]

Thus, religious portraits of women are similar to their social portraits. Positively depicted, women find their identity in belonging to someone else: father, husband, or sons. At worst, it is woman as thing, possession, and chattel; at best, it is woman as object of benevolent paternalism. One of the best examples of this paternalism at work is found in the concept of the "perfect wife" within classical Hindu Brahmanism. In this concept, husbands are gods and spiritual leaders and teachers (gurus) for their wives, and the one devotional practice for wives is devotion to their husband: When women perform ritual vows or acts of penance (vrats) or acts of devotion (bhakti), it is usually not for themselves but for their husbands and children.[28] Even those holy women who leave the domestic scene and their husbands to devote themselves to a god are nevertheless caught in the ideal of the "perfect wife." They simply exchange devotion and marriage to a human husband for devotion and marriage to a god.[29]

To understand the interplay of social and religious influences in the marginalization of women, it may be necessary to investigate other factors. Victoria Bernal's study of the development of a fundamentalist or text-based understanding of Islam in a Sudanese village, Wad al Abbas, illustrates a clear link between the marginalization of women and a particular combination of social, economic, and religious forces. Bernal outlines what happens in the village when many of the men begin to travel to Saudi Arabia as migrant workers. The men's lives and their knowledge and experience of the outside world change dramatically with the new economic order, and, as a result of what they have experienced in Saudi Arabia, the village makes a connection subsequently between Islamic fundamentalism and the "good life."[30]

Thus there develops in Wad al Abbas a new understanding of what constitutes Islam, which has repercussions for the life of the women in the village. Their lives become more and more limited to the domestic sphere, and more restricted by the imposition of new forms of seclusion and modesty that the men have seen operating in Saudi Arabia.[31] While the women have remained in the village and retained continuity with how the world was before the new order, unfortunately for them, the link with past tradition that was previously seen as positive is judged now to be "backward," "ignorant," and "irreligious."[32]

THE DEEPER STRUCTURES OF MARGINALIZATION: WOMEN'S BODIES

While you work through this section, I would like you to keep in mind the kinds of questions posed earlier in this chapter about the language that traditions offer to women to speak of their experience. I want to investigate here the kinds of language that religious traditions use about women, in particular about women's bodies or about what women's bodies do and the effects they have. I will begin with the view of a woman's body as a place of danger and shame, together with the powerful associated concept of taboo and the control of women's bodies, including the ultimate controlling idea that full religious membership or salvation for women can be achieved only by a change of sex. I will move from there to the broader canvas of theology, investigating how theology works out of anthropology and hence out of the view of women as defined by their bodies. Finally, I will consider the deeper issue of the alienation of a woman from her body-self in activity characterized as spiritual sado-masochism.

Women's Bodies as Dangerous

In this first section, I want to consider two ways in which women's bodies can be dangerous for religious traditions: first, women's bodies as powerful and sexually alluring; second, women's bodies as a danger to male or family honor. I will also look at the onus put on women to be responsible for men's morality.

In religious traditions in general, it is quite clear that women's bodies are problematical. As I wrote in chapter 2, the religious institutional answers to the question, "What is a woman?," often focus on the biological and social life-stages of women. In comparison with stories, teaching, and practices relating to men, those dealing with women are almost totally focused on women's bodies and their phases related to fertility—when they become fertile (onset of menstruation) or officially able to breed (marriage), when they have produced evidence of fertility (birth), when they are past the age of childbearing (menopause), or have lost their husbands (widowhood).

Thus, the discourse about women in religions is almost totally one-dimensional, based on gender and sexual function. The same does not apply to the discourse about men. Let me give one small example from the categorization of Roman Catholic saints. Women saints are categorized, for the most part, as virgins, martyrs, holy women (read the last category as "married"), and queens. The men saints are never categorized as virgins but as martyrs, priests (i.e., religious professionals), abbots, bishops, popes (i.e., administrators and powerful men), confessors of the faith, doctors of the church (i.e., scholars and teachers), kings, and so on.

Women are generally presented in positive or negative light by the traditions according to their attitude and behavior in relation to their own sexual potential and how the religious tradition proposes to deal with it. The ideal woman then is one who either is not theoretically a sexually active being (i.e., virgin, widow) or can be controlled sexually (i.e., wife, mother). These are the key themes again and again in the religious literature and the stories dealing with women, producing an overwhelming portrait of what it is that constitutes the best a woman can be.

Of the positive roles, the most desirable is the woman who is sexually controlled in marriage, since she provides a legitimate focus and channel for men's sexual desire, and, most importantly, the potential for raising men's status by producing sons for them. However, in some traditions, the reward for women in this most positive role can be a time of taboo or uncleanness. Thus, within Hinduism, a woman who bears a son may be auspicious while at the same time being polluted through childbirth.[33]

The contrast to the ideal woman is usually provided by the sexually active woman outside of familial systems of control (the prostitute). Thus, there are usually two roles for women in religious discourse—evil seductress or docile virgin/wife. Within Hinduism, Julia Leslie illustrates from Tryambaka the view that women are inherently wicked and must become perfect wives in order to be transformed.[34] In the Christian tradition, the two most popular images have been the virgin or saint and the whore. Virgins deny the body completely and gain heavenly reward; whores give in to desire or lust completely and are damned. It is no accident that through the history of the Christian tradition, perhaps especially within the Catholic stream, the two most powerful and reflected-upon characters have been the Virgin Mary and the (erroneously categorized) sinner/whore Mary Magdalen. This kind of discourse presents a terrible conundrum for Christian women. On the one hand, sexual activity is seen as tainted; on the other hand, Christianity presents women's fulfillment in terms of motherhood (see, e.g., 1 Tim. 2:15—". . . woman will be saved through bearing children, if she continues in faith and love and holiness, with modesty"). The solution lies in the humanly impossible image of Mary, who is both virgin and mother.

At this stage, I clearly need to ask what problem exists that makes it necessary to expend so much energy on control, either in practice or discourse. Why should men be afraid of women's bodies? The very fact of fear implies that women's bodies are powerful in some way. There are a great variety of views across religions and cultures about the mysterious and dangerous qualities of women, especially in relation to their sexuality, and the power it has to give life or bring death or sickness.[35] The source of these views is often to be found far back in the history of these religions and cultures, in an earlier understanding or appreciation of the power present in a woman's ability to produce life or in the power she seems to have in the constant renewal of herself in the cyclical shedding of blood without dying or being weakened as a man might be in shedding blood.

In her classic work, *Purity and Danger*, Mary Douglas points out that all margins are dangerous,[36] so one must consider the impact of the bodily emissions of women together with those from men. Yet, it is clear that the uncontrollable and frequent emissions that cross the margins of a woman's body, especially emissions of blood, are often considered by religions to have considerably more power and thus more danger attached to them. As Marglin points out for Hinduism, menstruation and childbirth are sources of impurity because they involve bodily fluids crossing the boundaries of the body, in the same way as with wounds or bodily wastes or bodily emissions. Men are less impure than women because their bodies are the source of fewer conditions of impurity.[37]

One finds taboos related to the female conditions of menstruation and childbirth, for example, in Chinese religion, in Japanese Shinto religion, and in orthodox Judaism, as well as in the religious life of many small-scale forager or village societies. Although there is no formal taboo in Christianity, the old rulings about a woman not being allowed to enter the sanctuary of a Christian church, where the altar is located, surely go back to the Jewish taboos against contact with menstruating women and their restriction from access to sacred cultic space.

The English term *taboo* is of Pacific island origin, first noted by Captain Cook. R.R. Marett suggests that the terms *tabu* (Tongan), *tapu* (Polynesian), *tabu* and *tambu* (Melanesian), and *kapu* (Hawaiian) mean literally "marked off." Applying to either persons or things, the state of taboo marks off that person or thing from ordinary or common existence by virtue of the relationship it has with extraordinary power either temporarily or permanently. It also sends a warning to others that it is extremely dangerous to treat such a person or thing in a casual fashion.[38]

In the original context of the Pacific religions, the extraordinary power behind taboo is *mana*, which incorporates ideas of both power and luck. It is abstract power and in a sense unstable, since one cannot be certain how it might react or with what degree of force. Marett likens it to "spiritual electricity that must be insulated lest it blast the unwary."[39] Thus, a person who is taboo is polluted with a power that is extremely risky for the community and against which the community must protect itself or which the community must find some way of channeling in a positive manner to its advantage.

Kalpana Ram's study of Mukkuvar women, in their heavily Hindu-influenced Catholic community in India, illustrates the point well. In describing the rituals of the community surrounding menarche and childbirth, she deals with the idea that a woman's body and its processes open her more easily than men to dangerous supernatural forces, with the result that a woman in such a state must be contained, secluded, and controlled to prevent possession and subsequent pollution and danger to the community. Moveover, the woman is also a threat to herself because her heat and blood attract supernatural forces.[40]

Of course, everyone in the community has *mana* to a certain extent, but systems of taboo regulate unequal degrees of *mana* so that those with a greater degree can be kept at a safe distance from those with less.[41] Thus, taboos are about establishing order and status in a particular community, while controlling potentially chaotic extraordinary power that resides in sacred polluted objects or people.

The fact that the power suffusing the thing or person that is taboo may cause either damage or benefit when tampered with indicates that there is a degree of ambiguity in the value of a taboo, and some religious systems mirror this by categories of taboo. However, negative or positive categories of taboo are equally states possessed of *mana*, not two different types of taboo.

The concept of taboo when applied to women may be rather ambiguous. Within a particular system, women may seem to have very little social or cultic power, and yet, at the same time, may be thought to possess uncontrollable extraordinary power. One of the major aspects of taboo as applied to women is the attempt to control this potentially chaotic and risky extraordinary power. I would suggest that this concept of taboo lies at the heart of the fear of women's sexuality in the major religions and their labeling of it as risky, uncontrolled, and in need of restriction and control, whether that is expressed formally by a term like taboo or not.

The difficulty for women with regard to this concept is that at some stage in the history of religious traditions, there appears to be a move from the idea of the taboo state as one of pollution with extraordinary power to one of pollution per se. A shift occurs from the idea of taboo as "marked off" and polluted to taboo as unworthy, irreligious, dirty, shameful, and profane in relation to the holiness perceived to reside in the formal aspects of religion as controlled by the professionals. Thus, blood shed outside of the controlled shedding of blood either literally or metaphorically in the space and time of sanctioned cultic practice is not powerful but simply dirty and unworthy. As one of my students, Lesley-Ann Leavoy, wrote: "It's better to bleed culturally than naturally." I would alter that to read, "It's better to bleed cultically than naturally."

It is above all in the cult that women's dangerous state of impurity or sexual potency is thought to have its effect. The cyclical, uncontrolled possession of women by extraordinary power makes others afraid, especially those responsible for the controlled cultic situations in which extraordinary power is said to manifest or be called down. The result is that dangerous women must go to the margins, where they will have less effect. This is only common sense, since the community needs to avoid a conflict between the extraordinary power they seem able to control in cultic practice and the same extraordinary power that is unstable and unpredictable within those who are taboo.[42]

Yet current practice in the major religions leads me to think

that the reasons for the exclusion of women from ritual and sacred space now relate more to unworthiness and impurity than
to any idea of power that resides within them—unless that be the
power of their seductiveness feared by male religious professionals, who find it difficult to resist the terrible nature of women's
sexuality. As Maitland claims for Christianity: "[F]emale sexuality
is always dangerous and usually wicked. It is not just self-destruc-
tive; it is dangerous to men."[43]

Thus, impurity is not just pollution and unworthiness but im-
morality and evil, and it is a very small step from this point to the
association of women with a devil figure or malevolent power. It
is therefore not surprising that there continues to be a discourse
of shame, not just in religious traditions but in the social context
as well, related to women's sexuality and their bodily processes
such as menstruation. Such processes linked to feelings of shame
can even result in women's exclusion from spiritual liberation.
The most extreme of the three sects of the Jains, the Digambaras,
say that women are more given to feelings of shame and modesty
than men. Since they are not able to overcome these feelings suf-
ficiently to be able to wander publicly in the nude, they cannot
undertake the wandering ascetic life that is open to men, and
thus cannot attain spiritual liberation immediately following life
in a female body.[44]

The literal meaning of taboo as "marked off" gives some feeling for the isolation that often accompanies this state. For women,
the isolation has been primarily into the domestic arena or marginal areas away from public social spaces. In a state of taboo,
women are often isolated into a community setting, for example,
all the currently menstruating women will be in the same place,
or are forced to remain only in those areas in the community
where women gather. I would propose, however, that the real
place of isolation is the body as the source of and reason for the
taboo. Childbirth and its aftermath and menstruation are often
experiences that move a woman back into herself with a concen-
tration on the forces at work, often painfully, in the body.

There is a strong sense of irony in the fact that the women who
are considered so powerful or so profane that they must be con-

trolled within the religious traditions often have very little control over the bodily processes that result in their pollution with
power or profaneness. Julie Marcus discusses this issue of the uncontrollable nature of women's pollution within Islam. Attempts
are made in this tradition to limit the danger women present, to
the extent that women are unable to perform the majority of the
activities that are at the heart of Muslim practice (called the Five
Pillars), unable to achieve the state of purity for prayer, fasting,
pilgrimage to Mecca, and reading the Qur'an.[45]

Marcus makes the general point about pollution that while men
also may be impure at certain times, they can voluntarily become
pure, but a woman's impurity is beyond her control.[46] Thus, a
woman's sexuality is seen as excessive, out of control unless controlled by a man to ensure the honor of the family (husband/
father).[47] Such men must constantly worry, for example, about
the virgins lest they lose their virginity (i.e., someone damages the
"property" belonging to the family). Women who wish to leave
the control of the family by getting a divorce are theoretically able
to do so, but as Elizabeth Fernea and Basima Bezirgan point out,
although such rights of women are protected in the Qur'an, the
lived experience is very different. A woman's demands for justice
can be easily overridden, or she can be pressured into not following through such a course of action because of some consideration of the family honor.[48]

There seems very little corresponding reflection in religious
traditions about men's degree of sexual control, or there is little
emphasis placed upon it. It may come as something of a surprise,
then, to hear or read of customs or laws that are clearly explicitly
designed for the gratification of men's uncontrollable sexual ap-
petite, such as the idea of temporary marriage (*mot'a*) within
Shi'ite Islam, which can cover anything from a quick trip to the
local prostitute to rape in war.[49]

Often, the idea of men's uncontrollable sexuality can only be
read implicitly in texts or teachings. As I mentioned above, the
Digambara sect of the Jains holds that women cannot be wandering ascetics, because of the nudity required for monastic
praxis. A number of reasons are given for this, one of which is

the supposed revulsion of those who might see a naked (and possibly menstruating) woman. Other reasons have more to do with men's uncontrollable behavior, such as the idea that women would inevitably have to live with a constant fear of sexual attack that would not give them the peace of mind necessary for the true spiritual path.

While women are supposed to be less controlled sexually then men, nevertheless they are inevitably made to be responsible for men's sexual reactions and forced to take a much higher moral stand than a man is expected to take. Such a double standard operates in many religious traditions. The Hebrew scriptures state that a woman must be a virgin at marriage (she can be stoned if not [Deut. 22:13–21]), and yet there is no expectation that this will be so for the husband (family honor/possessions are at stake—one needs to know that the sons born to the woman belong legitimately to her husband).

When women are considered to fail morally, they must take a greater punishment. Ironically, in attempting to be morally acceptable, they are also often expected to take greater punishment, for example, to commit suicide or to force violence against themselves, even murder, rather than allow themselves to be raped. I am reminded of the story of Maria Goretti, a young Italian girl who lived early in the twentieth century, who was stabbed and murdered because she would not give in to the sexual advances of a young man. She was held up to many young women in Catholic high schools as the ideal heroic type of Christian womanhood.

Rhetoric about heroism is also to be found in Islam in relation to women's greater moral responsibility. Barbara Stowasser characterizes fundamentalist Islam's view of the scriptural perspective on women who are "soldiers in a popular battle for communal righteousness. In her traditional role as loving wife and nurturing mother, the woman fights a holy war for the sake of Islamic values where her conduct, domesticity, and dress are vital for the survival of the Islamic way of life. Religion, morality, and culture stand and fall with her."[50]

Julie Marcus illustrates that the issue of control covers more than a general concern about women's sexuality. Loss of control of the body in menstruation and childbirth is considered among Muslims to indicate a general lack of emotional control. Women are open to irrationality and thus are unreliable spiritually. The general view among Muslims that women are too emotional and are controlled by passion rather than rationality adds to the reasons for their exclusion from any religious roles other than those available in their local indigenous, pre-Islamic practices.[51]

Exclusion from religious roles may rest on a broader base of difficulties than women's unreliable spirituality. Male religious professionals generally control the structure of, and policy relating to, religious ritual and roles for members. From the writings and behavior of such men, it seems clear that many have a difficulty with women, often exhibiting a fear of women's sexuality, viewing the woman as temptress and personification of desire. It seems to me that abuse of women by male religious professionals may also be partly occasioned by this fear of women's sexuality. A man may find a way out of the danger of entrapment or out of the fear by proving his power over what he is afraid of through conquering it by force.

The reason for the fear may be linked with some of the points that I have made above in this section, but there is one more aspect of women's sexuality that is sometimes considered dangerous by male professionals. Many religions view the use of sexual power as diminishing or distracting from spiritual or religious power, as a drain on an individual's spiritual energy. This is connected somewhat with the idea that women possess great power during sexual intercourse and may rob a man not only of physical strength but also of spiritual strength. Obviously, male religious professionals will be in a dangerous position if their spiritual power diminishes, so women are just as much a constant worry for the celibate Buddhist monk as for the Talmudic rabbi and for Christian priests.

The perception by male professionals of this potential danger finds expression in a number of ways—among them, very negative portrayals of women by male professionals, especially those espousing a monastic or celibate lifestyle. Fear of women may also lead male professionals to demand that women deny their sexuality in order to pursue a path of holiness or spiritual liberation. The extreme situation of a change of sex may be judged necessary for women to reach full communication or unity with extraordinary power.[52] Perhaps the most well-known example for the Christian tradition comes from the conclusion of the *Gospel of Thomas*, logion 114:

> Simon Peter said to them: Let Mary go forth from among us, for women are not worthy of the life. Jesus said: Behold, I shall lead her, that I may make her male, in order that she also may become a living spirit like you males. For every woman who makes herself male shall enter into the kingdom of heaven.[53]

Sometimes, a kind of sex change is considered to have taken place in women who choose a life of virginity within a tradition. Katharina Wilson cites the example of the early Christian saint Jerome who writes, in his commentary on the Letter to the Ephesians (3:5), that virginity raises women to equality with men because by espousing virginity, they cease to be women. A married woman, by her function of bearing children, is different from a man as the body is different from the soul, "but when she wishes to serve Christ more than the world, then she will cease to be a woman and will be called man."[54]

Those who follow a path of celibate holiness, then, are somehow seen to be doing something essentially male. A good example of this way of thinking is given by Margaret Smith, who quotes 'Attar, the biographer of the Muslim saint Rabi'a: "When a woman walks in the way of God like a man, she cannot be called a woman." 'Attar also likens Rabi'a to "a second spotless Mary."[55] Like the Virgin Mary, she has denied her female sexuality and taken on the male qualities of holiness, religious longing, and devotion. In relation to this idea of holiness connected to a loss of female sexuality, Fatima, Muhammad's daughter, is said to have been free from the deficiency of menstruation in order to devote herself to prayer and fasting.[56]

Women's Bodies and Theology About Women

In the section above on social and religious margins, I spoke of the way in which both religious traditions and societies collaborate in their views of men and women by virtue of sexual difference. I want to take that idea a little further here. Whatever way a society has of talking about and imaging sexual difference, religions generally can be seen to theologize on this discourse.

The realm of the sacred mirrors the human realm. There are theological myths of sexual power and abasement that clearly mirror the prevailing social view. Some Gnostic myths provide good illustrations of this process. The Gnostics have a number of myths to account for the entrapment of the divine Light in the evil material world. I have already outlined the one in which Sophia is the main female character. Another myth is found in *The Exegesis of the Soul*. In this text the soul is portrayed as a female entity, the spouse of the high heavenly God. She is pursued and raped by the evil heavenly powers (the archons) and consequently in her distress forgets who her real heavenly spouse is and becomes trapped in the world. She must wait until God sends her heavenly brother to rescue her before the Light can be restored. This is theology based on a story of debasement and devaluing of the female.

In the case both of Sophia and of this story about the soul, the myth that is meant to be at the basis of an entire theological system is expounded in terms of the essential weakness of a female that causes the grief of the world. Either the female is so weak that she is easily overcome and raped, or she is overcome by her own desire, as Sophia was. This is not something especially new to the Gnostics; one of the sources for their interpretation is the already well-established story about Eve in the Book of Genesis in the Jewish scriptures, and its subsequent interpretation by Jewish scholars prior to the formation of Gnostic groups in the early centuries CE.

This is theology that finds its basis in a perception of women as weak, submissive, and easily swayed to irrationality by their desires. I have spoken of this to an extent already when I wrote of the social perception of women that lies behind their role as shamans in the North Thailand spirit cults. There are also aspects of theologizing about women that find their basis in views of women as powerful, in the sense of manipulative or threatening. These women are usually the monstrous figures of religious myth—fierce Kali, or Lilith who denies the demands of the Jewish God that she submit to Adam and thus becomes the monstrous woman of Jewish folktales.

Perhaps the most extreme example of theologizing about women's bodies—where theologizing processes go so far as to invent a type of body—can be found among the Jains. I have spoken already of the Digambara sect of the Jains. This sect does not allow women into its monastic orders and does not believe that women can achieve liberation from the cycle of rebirths (*moksha*) until they are reborn as men. This fact in itself is not so unusual when one compares what other religions have taught or come close to teaching at various stages in their history, but it is the Digambaras' explanation of why this is so that is interesting.

To explain why women cannot experience salvation, the Digambaras have created an imaginary female microbiology. They state that portions of a woman's body—especially orifices or indentations (genitals, space between the breasts, navel, armpits)—all give rise to vast numbers of minute organisms, sometimes rising specifically from bodily fluids. These organisms are destroyed by the ordinary activities of women, but this thereby involves women in injuring living beings, an activity abhorrent to the Jains who, like their founder Mahavira, practice extreme asceticism and follow a way of noninjury to any and all living beings. Moreover, the beings in the genitals cause a sort of "itching" that can only be relieved through intercourse, so women are never free from the sexual desires that block spiritual progress.[57]

Oddly enough, there is no complementary microbiology for men, so they are both free from causing harm to microbes and, if they do not engage in sex, are not partners with women in this massive destruction. Thus, the Digambara debate about the spiritual liberation of women focuses specifically on the biophysical nature of the human female, and female reproductive physiology is cited as a principal reason for the alleged incapacity of women to achieve spiritual liberation from the cycle of rebirths.

In the case study in chapter 1, I presented a similar example of a tradition that uses theology about women's bodies to exclude them, not so much from salvation, but from full participation in the structures of power in which male professionals function. It is clear, both in that example and in the case of the Digambaras, that assumptions are being made about what a woman is and what a man is, and perceptions of a woman by virtue of her biology are being used as a basis for theology or for making policies about the functioning of women within the institutional structures of a religious tradition.

Alienation Complete: Spiritual Sado-masochism and Systems of Abuse

I have borrowed the term "spiritual sado-masochism" from Sara Maitland, who discusses such activity in the lives and practices of a number of Christian saints (Rose of Lima, Mariana Paredes y Flores, Margaret Mary, Teresa of Avila), where the women acted out terrible bodily abuse upon themselves or used imagery about abuse even to the extent of the image of being raped by their lover God.[58] Reading Maitland's work forces me to ask if such violence is acted out by women upon themselves because of what their tradition has taught them about their bodies. Granted that such activity was/is not always limited to women—since both men and women are affected by the way in which religious traditions make sharp distinctions between nature/matter/bodies and spirit—nevertheless there are other factors at work—such as the woman's view of a male God as a powerful and overpowering lover in sharply defined sexual imagery—that can make the experience of women in this regard more complicated.[59]

The system that supports an individual's abuse of her own body can also support abuse of her by others who have power over her by virtue of the system at work both in the tradition and in its social context. God as supreme male with power over all is the role model for other males with power over a woman—perhaps her husband and her religious minister. Within such a system, each of these males may feel he has the right to abuse her by virtue of the position he has over her.[60]

Thus, male religious professionals may simply be part of the entire system of oppression and abuse that women experience, and the incidents of intentional abuse of women in which some male religious professionals are involved are often covered up by their male colleagues in silence and collusion as similar incidents are covered up by males in other social groups. To challenge the silence and collusion is to challenge, by implication, the entire religious system.

Maitland's view is not agreeable to all. Caroline Walker Bynum suggests that the activity of making one's own body suffer may indicate a woman's view of her body as a means or instrument toward spiritual development. Making the body suffer is not to deny it but to explore it for religious meaning. Bynum illustrates her point with the Italian saint Angela of Foligno, who found the taste of pus (from sick bodies) "as sweet as communion."[61]

As Philip Mellor points out, this use of the body cannot apply in Buddhism. Images of mutilation and suffering of female bodies as well as of male bodies in Buddhist stories and teaching are there for the sole aim of teaching absolute detachment from the body rather than the use of the body as a means to holiness or enlightenment.[62]

CONCLUSION

I have covered quite a number of issues in this chapter: the means women have for speaking of their religious experience and the problem of finding a language for speaking; the language that we might use as people who want to listen to and dialogue with these women; the authority that both religious traditions and the academic community have over the perception, categorization, and relating of women's religious experience; and finally, the marginalization strategies that religious traditions employ, either intentionally or unintentionally, in relation to women.

Not all women would consider that what I have presented within the section on marginalization strategies is necessarily negative, or in need of criticism or change, and I will deal with this particular issue in chapter 5. Suffice it to say here that there are some relatively positive aspects that might be found in marginal experience. I would suggest, for example, that women's experience on the edge of a tradition has increased the opportunity and incentive for dialogue with women on the edges of other traditions. It is as if women have simply turned away from looking at the center to looking outward beyond the edge on which they stand and have found other women looking back toward them from the edges of their own traditions. Dialogue at the edge with those of other traditions can be both supportive on a personal and group level and instructive in the analysis of strategies of power and manipulation at work across traditions.

The view of women's religious experience as marginal proceeds from an idea about religions that places religious professional people and the structures, rituals, and paraphernalia that support them in the central position. It is an idea that raises the basic question of what is religion. Granted that religious professionals and all that pertains to them are an indispensable part of how any religion survives and maintains membership, the question remains whether this indispensable part must also be the central part of every investigation into what being religious means.

In the following chapter, I take up the issue of woman as subject and center of the hermeneutical process, which I have already discussed in the preface and chapter 1. I will attempt to set women's religious experience in the center of our vision so that we might see and listen more effectively within the dialogue.

NOTES

1. Sheila Briggs, "Sexual Justice and the 'Righteousness of God,' " in Linda Hurcombe, ed., *Sex and God: Some Varieties of Women's Religious Experience* (New York: Routledge & Kegan Paul, 1987), p. 254.

2. Briggs, "Sexual Justice," p. 257.

3. Several years ago, an Australian aboriginal woman who came to speak to one of my classes about her aboriginal spirituality stated that she was not able to speak as openly as she would have wished because there was a male student present.

4. Frédérique Apffel Marglin, "Female Sexuality in the Hindu World," in Clarissa W. Atkinson et al., eds., *Immaculate and Powerful: The Female in Sacred Image and Social Reality* (Wellingborough, U.K.: Crucible, 1987), pp. 39–40. See the critical overview of Marglin's work in Glenn Yocum, "Burning 'Widows,' Sacred 'Prostitutes,' and 'Perfect Wives': Recent Studies of Hindu Women," *Religious Studies Review*, vol. 20 (1994), p. 280. Penny Magee ("Sex and Secularism: Indian Women and the Politics of Religious Discourse," in Morny Joy and Penny Magee, eds., *Claiming Our Rites: Studies in Religion by Australian Women Scholars*, Adelaide: AASR, 1994, pp. 157–85), too, calls for a reevaluation of indigenous traditions in relation to women rather than an emphasis on sacred texts and Hindu attitudes. Sandra Robinson ("Hindu Paradigms of Women: Images and Values," in Yvonne Yazbeck Haddad and Ellison Banks Findly, eds., *Women, Religion, and Social Change,* Albany: State University of New York Press, 1985, pp. 181–216) takes a slightly different tack and presents two alternate paradigms in Hinduism in relation to women: the Brahmanical, which focuses on goddesses and feminine nature, the ideal wife, and the value of women; and women in devotional Hinduism, which has an alternative understanding and is indigenous in origin and pre-Brahmanical. The latter gives devotional roles to women and recognizes women's rites (*vratas*). "The two paradigms presented here point to two distinctive constructs of femininity that coincide and coexist in Hindu traditions" (p. 211).

The discussion is made more complex by scholarly arguments currently raging as to whether a line can be drawn between non-Brahmanical and Brahmanical religion or whether the distinction is illusory; see, e.g., C. J. Fuller, *The Camphor Flame: Popular Hinduism in Society in India* (Princeton, N.J.: Princeton University Press, 1992), pp. 24–28.

5. Leila Ahmed, "Women and the Advent of Islam," *Signs: Journal of Women in Culture and Society*, vol. 11 (1986), p. 679.

6. Andrew Kadel, *Matrology: A Bibliography of Writings by Christian Women from the First to the Fifteenth Centuries* (New York: Continuum, 1995), p. 21.

7. Sara Maitland ("Passionate Prayer: Masochistic Images in Women's Experience," in Hurcombe, *Sex and God*, pp. 125–40) warns that "the

underlying gynophobia is often at its most virulent when appearing to praise individual women," p. 132.

8. Hilde Hein, "Liberating Philosophy: An End to the Dichotomy of Spirit and Matter," in Ann Garry and Marilyn Pearsall, eds., *Women, Knowledge, and Reality: Explorations in Feminist Philosophy* (Boston: Unwin Hyman, 1989), p. 294.

9. Amina Wadud-Muhsin, *Qur'an and Woman* (Kuala Lumpur: Penerbit Fajar Bakti, 1992), p. 33.

10. Najah Manasra, "Palestinian Women: Between Tradition and Revolution," in Ebba Augustin, ed., *Palestinian Women: Identity and Experience* (London: Zed Books, 1993), p. 19.

11. Donald K. Swearer, *The Buddhist World of Southeast Asia* (Albany: State University of New York Press, 1995), pp. 14–15.

12. Tamil proverb quoted in Susan S. Wadley, ed., *The Powers of Tamil Women* (Syracuse, N.Y.: Maxwell School of Citizenship and Public Affairs, 1980), p. xiii.

13. Geoffrey Samuel, "The Body in Buddhist and Hindu Tantra: Some Notes," *Religion*, vol. 19 (1989), p. 206.

14. Denise Lardner Carmody, *Women and World Religions*, 2nd ed. (Englewood Cliffs, N.J.: Prentice-Hall, 1989), pp. 102–3.

15. Steven E. Ozment, *Protestants* (London: Fontana, 1993), pp. 154, 159.

16. I. Julia Leslie, "Essence and Existence: Women and Religion in Ancient Indian Texts," in Pat Holden, ed., *Women's Religious Experience* (London: Croom Helm, 1983), p. 103.

17. Shibani Roy, *The Status of Muslim Women in North India* (Delhi: B.R. Publishing, 1979), p. 108.

18. Julie Marcus, *A World of Difference: Islam and Gender Hierarchy in Turkey* (St. Leonards, NSW: Allen & Unwin, 1992), pp. 130–34.

19. Marcus, *World of Difference*, p. 132.

20. Augustine, *The Confessions*, in Whitney J. Oates, ed., *Basic Writings of Saint Augustine*, vol. 1 (New York: Random House, 1948), p. 74.

21. Christine Kondoleon, *Domestic and Divine: Roman Mosaics in the House of Dionysos* (Ithaca/London: Cornell University Press), 1995, p. 2.

22. Leonard Swidler, *Women in Judaism: The Status of Women in Formative Judaism* (Metuchen, N.J.: Scarecrow Press, 1976), p. 125.

23. 'Abdur Rahman Doi, *Women in Shari'ah (Islamic Law)*, revised and edited by Abdalhaqq Bewley (London: Ta-Ha, 1992), p. 1.

24. Susan S. Wadley, "Hindu Women's Family and Household Rites in a North Indian Village," in Nancy Falk and Rita Gross, eds., *Unspo-

ken Worlds: Women's Religious Lives in Non-Western Cultures (San Francisco: Harper & Row, 1980), p. 73.

25. Leslie, "Essence and Existence," p. 100.

26. See, e.g., Peter Phillimore, "Unmarried Women of the Dhaula Dhar: Celibacy and Social Control in Northwest India," *Journal of Anthropological Research*, vol. 47 (1991), pp. 331–50.

27. Richard Schechner, "Crossing the Water: Pilgrimage, Movement, and Environmental Scenography of the *Ramlila* of Ramnagar," in Bradley R. Hertel and Cynthia Ann Humes, eds., *Living Banaras: Hindu Religion in Cultural Context* (Albany: State University of New York Press, 1993), p. 63.

28. Kathryn Hansen, "Heroic Modes of Women in Indian Myth, Ritual and History: The *Tapasvini* and the *Virangana*," in Arvind Sharma and Katherine Young, eds., *The Annual Review of Women in World Religions*, vol. 2 (Albany: State University of New York Press, 1992), pp. 8–14.

29. David Kinsley, "Devotion as an Alternative to Marriage in the Lives of Some Hindu Women Devotees," *Journal of Asian and African Studies*, vol. 15 (1980), pp. 83–84.

30. Victoria Bernal, "Gender, Culture, and Capitalism: Women and the Remaking of Islamic 'Tradition' in a Sudanese Village," *Comparative Studies in Society and History*, vol. 36 (1994), pp. 49–51.

31. Bernal, "Gender," pp. 45–47.

32. Bernal, "Gender," p. 52.

33. Marglin, "Female Sexuality," p. 40.

34. I. Julia Leslie, *The Perfect Wife: The Orthodox Hindu Woman According to the "Strīdharmapaddhati" of Tryambakayajvan*, Oxford University South Asian Studies Series (New York: Oxford University Press, 1989), pp. 262–63, 272. This is also the point of discussion in Prabhati Mukherjee, *Hindu Women: Normative Models* (New Delhi: Orient Longman, 1978), p. vii.

35. There may be exceptions, of course, even within traditions in which we know this to be generally true. Thus, Frédérique Marglin (*Wives of the God-King: The Rituals of the Devadasis of Puri*, New York: Oxford University Press, 1985) cites the example of the Hindu *devadasis* (women dedicated to a god, who lived and performed rituals in a temple—the system died out after Indian independence in 1947), for whom celibacy rather than female sexuality was dangerous, because celibacy represented the heat or drought that burns up the earth, the opposite of fertility and renewal (pp. 53–54).

36. Mary Douglas, *Purity and Danger: An Analysis of Concepts of Pollution and Taboo* (Harmondsworth, U.K.: Penguin, 1970), p. 121.

37. Marglin, "Female Sexuality," p. 40.

38. R. R. Marett, "Tabu," in James Hastings, ed., *Encyclopaedia of Religion and Ethics*, vol. 12 (Edinburgh: T. & T. Clark, 1926), p. 181.

39. Marett, "Tabu," p. 183.

40. Kalpana Ram, *Mukkuvar Women: Gender, Hegemony and Capitalist Transformation in a Southern Indian Fishing Community* (Sydney: Allen and Unwin, 1991), p. 90.

41. See Roy Wagner, "Taboo," in Mircea Eliade, ed., *The Encyclopedia of Religion*, vol. 14 (New York: Macmillan, 1987), p. 233.

42. See Wagner, "Taboo," p. 235.

43. Maitland, "Passionate Prayer," p. 132.

44. Robert P. Goldman, "Foreword," in Padmanabh S. Jaini, ed., *Gender and Salvation: Jaina Debates on the Spiritual Liberation of Women* (Berkeley: University of California Press, 1991), pp. xix–xx.

45. Marcus, *World of Difference*, p. 76. Almsgiving is the fifth activity.

46. Marcus, *World of Difference*, p. 68–69.

47. Marcus, *World of Difference*, p. 82–86.

48. Elizabeth Warnock Fernea and Basima Qattan Bezirgan, eds., *Middle Eastern Women Speak*, The Dan Danciger Publication Series (Austin: University of Texas Press, 1977), p. xxiv.

49. Yann Richard, *Shi'ite Islam*, tr. Antonia Nevill (Cambridge: Blackwell, 1995), pp. 165–67.

50. Barbara Freyer Stowasser, *Women in the Qur'an, Traditions, and Interpretation* (New York: Oxford University Press, 1994), p. 7.

51. Marcus, *World of Difference*, p. 90.

52. There is a well-established idea within Hinduism that men might become female in order to worship the goddess or that they become female *in* the worship. Perhaps the most famous example of a man taking on a female role was Ramakrishna, who dressed as a woman and identified himself as Radha (wife of Visnu). Karin Kapadia (*Siva and Her Sisters: Gender, Caste, and Class in Rural South India*, Boulder, Colo.: Westview Press, 1995) considers the fact that only men are allowed to become possessed by the goddess Mariyamman—and that they have to "become female" first—to be a further marginalization of women, since men are allowed to be both female and male, whereas women are not given this freedom (p. 125).

53. Edgar Hennecke, Wilhelm Schneemelcher, and R. McL. Wilson, eds., *New Testament Apocrypha. Volume 1: Gospels and Related Writings* (Philadelphia: Westminster, 1963), p. 522.

54. Katharina M. Wilson, ed., *Medieval Women Writers* (Athens: University of Georgia Press, 1984), pp. x, xxiii n. 22.

55. Margaret Smith, "Rabi'a the Mystic," in Fernea and Bezirgan, *Middle Eastern Women Speak* (excerpted from Margaret Smith's *Rabi'a the Mystic and Her Fellow-Saints in Islam,* Cambridge: Cambridge University Press, 1928), p. 39.

56. Marcia K. Hermansen, "The Female Hero in the Islamic Religious Tradition," in Sharma and Young, *The Annual Review,* p. 117.

57. Goldman, "Foreword," pp. xx–xxi.

58. Maitland, "Passionate Prayer," p. 136.

59. Maitland, "Passionate Prayer," p. 128.

60. Of course, abuse by male religious professionals is not limited to traditions with an all-powerful male deity. June Campbell's (*Traveller in Space: In Search of Female Identity in Tibetan Buddhism,* London: Athlone, 1996) experience as a Western woman who trained as a Buddhist and became the sexual partner (*songyum*—lit. "secret mother") of her male spiritual guide (yogi-lama) illustrates the point well. She was warned after becoming involved "that any indiscretion in maintaining silence over our affair might lead to madness, trouble, *or even death*" (p. 102).

61. Caroline Walker Bynum, "The Female Body and Religious Practice in the Later Middle Ages," in Ramona Naddaff et al. eds., *Fragments for a History of the Human Body. Part 1* (New York: Zone, 1989), p. 246. See also Philip A. Mellor, "Self and Suffering: Deconstruction and Reflexive Definition in Buddhism and Christianity," *Religious Studies,* vol. 27 (1991), p. 57.

62. Mellor, "Self and Suffering," p. 59.

4

Voices from
Center Stage

—⟋m⟍—

I spoke in chapter 3 about textbooks on religion in relation to
women's experience. Books specifically devoted to the subject of
women and religion or spiritual writings by women themselves
are another matter entirely, generally leaving us with a broader
and more comprehensive canvas for study. Such books clarify the
difference between the classical teachings of religions and the
lived experience of women, contrasting the experience of male
power over the production and maintenance and administration
of religion in all its forms to the history/herstory of women in
their own particular religious contexts, public or private. They analyze the socially constructed binarism of public-private and the
subordination implied in relegating women to the private sphere
while also investigating the activities of women in the private
sphere in their positive aspects, the creative ways that women have
enhanced the sphere in which they have been allowed to operate. They outline the diversity of the aims, processes, and philosophies of contemporary women's movements and the effect this is
having on the criticism of religion(s). Certainly, one continues to

hear stories of abuse and marginalization, but women are also presented as visible participants in religious life, living creatively as spiritual fringe-dwellers, with independent religious lives both within and outside of established traditions.

In this chapter, I will focus both on the independent religious life of women and on the marginal situations that I presented in chapter 3. For the latter, I will attempt to place material in the center so that I can see and hear it better.[1] As I do this, you will recognize that I am following the method I suggested both in the introduction and in chapter 1; that is, I am taking seriously the possibility of allowing women to speak from the center of the stage as I listen to their stories about religious experience, however these stories are passed on to me.

Before I begin to move or to invite the marginal to the center, however, I should ask if there are women already in the center. In chapter 3, I dealt with women who appear to be at the center of traditions in professional roles and suggested we proceed with caution as we consider how they come to be there and whether the status they appear to have is actually illusory. There are many possible reasons some women may be in the center, and I will look at some of these briefly.

Apart from relatively new roles created for women in traditional religions, as well as female leadership of new religious movements,[2] there are some examples of women traditionally holding central roles. Youngsook Kim Harvey's study of six Korean women shamans of the twentieth century, for example, shows the very real influence these women have had in Korean society at all levels: on royalty and ordinary people, on men and women, in both the public and the private domains. While, ordinarily, women in Korean society would have no authority—being under the control of fathers, husbands, or sons—shamans may choose whether to marry and need no formal institutionalized training to practice. As Harvey summarizes, "the role of shaman alone apparently offered women of traditional Korea the possibility of combining a professional career with family life."[3]

Women may hold central roles in reality but go unrecognized in fact both by the tradition and by academia. In chapter 3, I spoke of the study by Victoria Bernal of the experience of the people in Wad al Abbas. Because many men are migrant workers and thus are away from the village on a routine basis, women have come to control many ceremonies and rites of passage. Bernal reports that women control the frequent socio-ritual events, whereas men control the infrequent "major life crisis rituals" and the Friday mosque attendance.[4] While it appears, then, that women actually control a good deal of the religious life of the village and that their religious life should not be considered fringe in this context, I would almost guarantee that if my students took their model of Islam from the information in their required textbook or any other similar current textbook on world religions, they would tend to regard the mosque and the major male-controlled rituals as of primary interest to a study of Islam in that village. I wonder how many scholars of religion would do the same.

The geographic location of women should also be taken into account when considering women's position in religious traditions that have an international membership. Women may have a more central role in one location than in another. Thus, Donald Swearer documents the change in status of Buddhist nuns (*bhikkunis*) according to location, describing the experience of those in Burma, who manage their own monasteries, collect morning alms, pursue higher Buddhist studies including Pali, and participate in "religio-cultural institutions and practices from which they are virtually excluded in Thailand, Laos and Cambodia."[5] Fatima Mernissi writes of Iranian women who though fully veiled have jobs, hold office, travel, run businesses, attend university, and work with men who are not their relatives, whereas Saudi women are totally segregated and cannot go out without their husbands, and so on.[6] Barbara Callaway and Lucy Creevey report that Muslim women in northern Nigeria are secluded immediately upon marriage (at 10 to 12 years of age), whereas women in Senegal are not veiled or secluded.[7]

Many of the women who find a place in the center belong to groups that have high status in the social context of the religious tradition or are related to men with high status within the tradition, as I noted in chapter 3. Would we ever have heard of Oudil, the daughter of the Baal Shem Tov, if her father had not been prominent in the European Jewish Hasidic tradition?

Women of high social status may have the leisure and the education to attain status as professionals or holy women within religious traditions because of the systems of power within which they hold their key roles. In her collection of photos of women in the Middle East from the nineteenth and early twentieth centuries, Sarah Graham-Brown includes a photo of Mahd-e Awliya, mother of Nasir el-Din, Shah of Iran, and a woman of tremendous political power. The Iranian chronicler Mo'ayeral-Mamalek describes how she held her own religious ceremonies and "on days of mourning, ladies would gather round the food table and she would then herself begin the recitation of the Quran. . . ."[8]

Not many women could aspire to a similar context, but many women nonetheless have achieved recognized holiness or sainthood or enlightenment without the support of a social—or religious—status position. Each of the major religious traditions at least knows of exceptional holy women.[9] Some are given power by holy men, as was Archanapuri Ma, disciple of the great Hindu spiritual guide Ramakrishna, who was chosen to succeed him on his death.[10] Others may have power, but not from the hands of those who normally wield power in a tradition. The Christian Irish saint Brigit was ordained as a bishop by the bishop Mel. As Mary Condren points out, while not denying the incident, some "Lives of Brigit" stress that Mel was "intoxicated with the grace of God."[11] In other words, it was not his fault that Brigit received the high status of bishop—the spirit of God was clearly to blame.

Although there is ambiguity in the central professional roles of women, there are nevertheless some advantages. I noted in the previous chapter the difficulty that some Buddhist nuns experience, yet the lifestyle of both Buddhist nuns and Christian nuns in the past at least presented an alternative to family life and marriage, as did the life of devotion to a god followed by some Hindu female saints like Mahadeviyakka, Lallesvari, and Mirabai.[12] Quite often, convents or monasteries of nuns have been the only places where women have had some degree of autonomy within the context of everyday life, even though both Buddhist and Christian nuns have generally been under some supervision by their male counterparts. Karma Lekshe Tsomo reports that some Asian Buddhist nuns count themselves lucky to be nuns so that they do not have to have babies, in which case perhaps ordination can be seen as more advantageous for women than for men.[13]

MOVEMENT FROM MARGIN TO CENTER

In the introductory chapter, I reflected on how a reader/listener might invite women to be subjects in the hermeneutical process of interpreting women's religious experience. I suggested some simple techniques, such as changing pronouns from "they/them" to "we/us" so that women might tell their own stories, or of imagining women who are secondary characters moving to center stage to tell the story from their own perspective—and noted that the women subjects might thereby tell a different story. Where a woman appears in a story only as a secondary figure or as one who does not speak, imagine that she moves to center stage and see the story unfold again from her point of view. Often, women are in the stories, but readers have neither seen them nor been listening for their voices.

Centering Women in Stories/Text

Let me give you some ideas of how you might use this technique. Roshi Philip Kapleau tells a Buddhist story from the Japanese Middle Ages that concerns a geisha and a Buddhist monk. The geisha receives news that her mother is seriously ill, but she does not have the money for the doctor's fee for a cure. She asks her drunken rich patron to lend her the money, and he replies that he will give her the money if she manages to seduce a pure-minded monk he knows of. She is received by the monastery as a stranger on a stormy night, and having used their bath, proceeds to try to seduce the monk, all to no avail. When she breaks down at her failure, she tells the monk the whole story and asks for his forgiveness. The monk invites her to go to bed with him.

When the abbot hears the next day what has happened, the monk is dismissed. However, his fellow monks plead on his behalf, saying that he has taught them a lesson in compassion. The story concludes with sayings about purity that we are obviously meant to see in the monk's behavior.[14]

Now if I invite the geisha to stand in the center and listen to her, what might she speak to me about? I imagine that she would tell me of her mother, of her love for her mother, of her desperation that her mother is ill, and of her unwillingness to do what her rich patron asks. If I listen to her carefully, I might decide that the story is not only about a monk's compassion and purity of intent but also about the geisha's compassion and purity of intent. So not only the monk but also the geisha can be a model for monks to learn what compassion and purity of intent mean. The geisha is also much lower in status than the monk within the religious and social hierarchy, so the story also tells me that those of lowly status can be models of purity as much as those of high status.

Sometimes it might be difficult to hear a woman's voice when she takes center stage. An example for me is the horrific story of the Levite's concubine in the Book of Judges 19 in the Jewish scriptures. The story tells of a concubine who leaves her husband, a Levite (i.e., a member of the Hebrew tribe of the Levites or priests), and returns to her father's house. The husband follows to retrieve her some months later and then sets out with her for his home. They stop for the night in a city belonging to the Hebrew tribe of the Benjaminites, and local men demand from their host that he send the Levite out so they can rape him. The host offers them instead both his daughter and the Levite's concubine, and the Levite pushes his concubine out the door to them. They rape and torture her all night, and in the morning she crawls back to the threshold of the door of the house. The Levite comes out to go on his way, sees her lying motionless, presumably dead, with her hands on the threshold, puts her on his donkey, takes her home, and proceeds to cut her into twelve pieces to send around the country of Israel to show the horror of what was done by the Benjaminites.

When I invite the concubine to come to center stage and speak about the events of the story from her point of view, I introduce a personal level to the story that is clearly not the main aim of its telling in the context of the Book of Judges. In that context, she is a political symbol for Israel in its disintegration under a tribal system that desperately needs a king to restore order. In fact, most conventional biblical commentaries will speak of the woman only in this way. When I attempt to hear the concubine speak personally rather than as a political symbol, I am often so overwhelmed by the horror of her story that I can only either listen to her weep or simply sit beside her broken body. There may be other things I can do, once I have tried to hear her speak. Perhaps I can invite other women of her time and culture to come and speak on her behalf.

In both the Jewish and the Buddhist stories above, I have added another perspective to the way in which they are most frequently presented within their respective traditions. Sometimes this technique may actually cause the reader to come into conflict with earlier interpretations. Muhammad's wife Aisha has frequently been used by Muslim theologians as an example of why women should not have any power, since they attribute the split in Islam between the two major streams of the tradition, Sunni and Shi'ite, and the consequent violence and suffering, to the battles Aisha fought, literally and politically. Fatima Mernissi comes into conflict with this view when she reinterprets Muhammad's wives, Aisha included, as "dynamic, influential, and enterprising members of the community, and fully involved in Muslim public affairs."[15]

Other retellings/rereadings may come into conflict with aspects of a tradition that are basic to its structure. Let me take the example of the First Letter to Timothy 2:11–12 within the Christian scriptures, which reads, "Let a woman learn in silence with full submission. I permit no woman to teach or to have authority over a man; she is to keep silent." Together with similar "hard sayings" about women in the scriptures, these verses form the basis for some groups to argue against allowing any significant role in ritual or decision-making to women Christians.

I invite the women who belong to the community addressed
by this letter to take center stage. They might tell me that the
community has been having trouble with some people spreading
false teaching (4:1–5; 6:2–5). Some of the women have listened
to the false teachers and turned away from the true faith (5:13,15).
Someone in the community has written about this to the community founder/leader who is away, and the leader has written
back to issue a blanket command forbidding women to teach or
have authority. The leader is concerned, of course, to limit the
damage already done. Since the leader does not know which
women have been affected by the false teaching, the best short-
term remedy is to stop any woman from teaching, presuming of
course that the false teachers themselves have moved on. They
might also tell me that this short-term remedy was only in place
until the leader's return and that things returned to normal, as
far as women's teaching and positions of authority were concerned, once the community had dealt with the dangerous situation of the false teaching. They might also express surprise that
instructions in a letter by their leader, addressed specifically to
their particular local situation, should have become a general di-
rective for the entire church and a key source for marginalizing
women from teaching and holding office in the Christian tradition. They might suggest that I listen to their sisters in Corinth
(1 Cor. 11:5) or Caesarea (Acts 21:9), who clearly enjoyed the
privileges of speaking, teaching, presiding over ritual, and pray-
ing in the worshipping community.

   That is one possible scenario from listening to the women's
voices. There might be another entirely. The women might speak
about how there had been some tension in the community concerning leadership roles for men and women and about how those
who did not want women to have leadership roles had gained a
position of greater strength. As part of their strategy for limiting
the voice of women in such roles, they had brought notice to the
community that some women had been spreading false teaching.
At this stage of community development, there was such an emphasis upon community cohesiveness and the need for all to follow the true teaching that the mere charge was enough for the

community leader/founder to write and forbid women from teaching or having authority over men. The women might tell me, too, that what happened in their community was happening elsewhere, until eventually all the Christian communities that claimed to follow the "true teaching" were united in denying women any leadership roles at all.

Rereading texts with the women at center stage can be a complex activity. Itumeleng Mosala suggests that in her reading of the Book of Esther from the Jewish scriptures in relation to African women's struggle in South Africa, she is weaving together human, African, and feminist hermeneutics of liberation. As a South African woman she struggles against oppression on a number of levels; her struggle is at once against gender, national, and class oppression.

Mosala's study of the Book of Esther is most interesting because in this text a woman is already center stage, or appears to be. Mosala's reading provides a lesson about being cautious of the appearance of status given to women in stories. Her analysis finds that the female character has simply been used to achieve what are basically patriarchal ends. Mosala uses the story to comment on her own experience as a South African woman:

> The fact that the story is woven around Esther does not make her the heroine. The hero of the story is Mordecai who needlessly to say gives nothing of himself for what he gets. . . . African women who work within liberation movements and other groups will be very familiar with these kinds of dynamics.[16]

In the stories above, I have invited as speakers women who normally are not seen to be the key characters in the text. Although the women may be central to the action, they have subordinate roles in the texts: the geisha is there to highlight the qualities of the monk, the concubine is there to illustrate a political problem, and the women in the Christian community are there because of the apparent problem that they are causing.

Amina Wadud-Muhsin comments from her Muslim perspective: "In other religions, feminists have had to insert woman into the discourse in order to attain legitimacy. The Muslim woman has only to read the text—unconstrained by exclusive and restrictive interpretations—to gain an undeniable liberation."[17] I disagree with Wadud-Muhsin's blanket comment. I have not inserted the women in the stories; they are already there. Many have simply not been allowed to speak until now, or readers have not bothered to listen. However, I think that what I have done in centering the women by inviting them to speak is something akin to what Wadud-Muhsin proposes—a reading of the stories in such a way that I am not constrained by more traditional and restrictive interpretations.

Centering Women's Experience in Domestic/Private Space

Of course, not all streams of a religious tradition may find woman's place in the home. Women in monastic orders are encouraged to give up family life and to concentrate their lives on the path of holiness or enlightenment, unencumbered by children and spouse. Yet even within the home, religions have made room for women to have some religious significance. Though generally lower in status within a tradition, when a domestic space is made holy by some ritual—and some traditions such as Hinduism have extensive domestic ritual—then it is likely that women will be the central actors in the ritual, whether that be in lighting the Sabbath candles for the weekly Jewish ritual of worship or in lighting each night the oil lamps that symbolize the Hindu goddess Lakshmi. In fact, Christopher Fuller states that, although women's inferior status within Hinduism always permeates the performance and participation in religious activity, nevertheless women perform ritual more often, and thus they are considered to have more ritual power (*shakti*).[18]

Women may also have a central role in the early socialization/education of children into a tradition. Thus, the home as primarily women's space may exert considerable influence upon a tradition, a fact often acknowledged implicitly by religious traditions in which male children are taken from the home at a young age to be placed into the care of male religious professionals for training.

When I read textbooks on world religions now, and see how they focus mainly on the public life of religions in which men are involved as central actors, I begin to wonder what they are not telling me about the religious life of the women. I want to invite the women to take center stage and ask them: What does it mean to you as a Jewish woman to prepare the meal for the Sabbath (*shabbat*) while the menfolk go off to synagogue? If, as a Jewish woman, you rarely go to synagogue on shabbat, do you miss not going? Is the synagogue the center of meaning for your religious life? What do you as a Muslim woman do when the men go off to the mosque? If, as a Muslim woman, you never go, or rarely go, to the mosque, do you miss it? You are constantly reminded of the mosque in the religious culture around you, but is the mosque truly the center of your religious life?

Women themselves may transform their homes or domestic duties into a center for extraordinary power, into alternative constructed sacred spaces. Writings by and about women give some indication of the information that is lacking in traditional textbooks on this aspect of women's lives. In *The Three Pillars of Zen*, for example, there is the story of an American schoolteacher who goes on a Zen Buddhist retreat (*sesshin*) with her husband and three children. Both adults take part in the meditations, while alternating in looking after the children. The woman relates that she and her husband both achieved spiritual awakening (*kensho*).[19]

Sacred spaces in the home may be temporary, as with specific home rituals. Julie Marcus and Shibani Roy deal with rituals held in the home by Muslim women, including the ritual of *mevlüt*, which is held forty-seven to fifty-two days after a person's death and then annually thereafter.[20] The structure of the rituals usually involves a gathering of women of various statuses, readings, performances by male Muslim teachers or sometimes women, and ritual weeping, with a meal following.

Sacred spaces may also be permanent. Cynthia Ann Humes tells of Rama Rani Maharotra, who established the temple of the Hindu goddess Vindhyavasini in her home in 1975 after receiving the gift of channeling the goddess's healing powers.[21] Manisha Roy gives more general detail of the way in which middle-aged Hindu Bengali women can choose a spiritual guide (*guru*) and lead a religious life of full-time religious activities. Such a woman can spend a great deal of time with her guru, worshiping him as her god and often finding more emotional satisfaction in this relationship than in the relationship with her husband.[22] It seems, then, that women in later life—at least in Bengal—may have better access to the spiritual life than men, who in middle age continue to work and provide for the family.

I have dealt with the transformation of the home in the examples above. The reverse is found in the idea that by establishing the domestic sphere in good order, one establishes religion. Madeleine Tress tells the story of the occupation of the Park Hotel in Hebron on April 4, 1968, by sixty Israelis posing as Swiss tourists, intending to reclaim the Jewish quarter. The women immediately cleaned and prepared the hotel kitchen for the cooking of kosher Jewish food as a first step in the reclamation of the Jewish quarter.[23] The domestic aspect of religion is the prerequisite for ordered religious institutional life.

Finally, in this section I should sound a note of caution. Though I am celebrating here women as central actors in the sacred space of the home, I have already spoken in chapter 3 of how that space may be a place of abuse for women rather than a sacred place. To celebrate women as central actors does not mean that I should not also critique the fact that women are sometimes restricted to this space as the most meaningful that a tradition can find for them.

I need to be careful also about the kind of rhetoric that is becoming more predominant in both religious and political or social language, about a return to "family values." As Bonnie Miller-McLemore writes, ". . . the term *family values* has become a distorted and sometimes politically dangerous code word for reinstituting male dominance and female self-sacrifice."[24] Mother-

hood can be viewed as an essential aspect of women by both radical feminists and antifeminists alike, with very different outcomes.

Centering the Concepts About Women's Sexuality and the Need to Control It

I began in this chapter with centering activity in relation to texts
and stories about women. I can also analyze some of the terms
and models used within religious traditions to talk about women's
religious experience and do something with these similar to what
I have done with the stories. I dealt with the concept of taboo in
chapter 3 as an implicit or explicit marginalizing device used for
controlling the danger inherent in women's sexuality. When inviting women who are taboo to take center stage, I may do a number of things: I may ask them to speak of what they have experienced in that state, how they understand it themselves, and how
they have been creative spiritually within that space; and I may
ask about the early meaning of taboo and how I may reappreci-
ate that concept in relation to women's religious lives.

   In her book, *Women and World Religions*, Denise Lardner Carmody retells Lis Harris' story of having attended a ritual bath fre-
quented by Jewish women for purification after childbirth or menstrual period, and she paints a picture of real community and life
among the women.[25] I was surprised when I first read this story
because up to that point, I had seen purification rituals like these
only as impositions and restrictions, as negative rituals. From Carmody's story, I began to glimpse another possibility, to appreciate a religious life of women that cannot be understood solely in
negative terms, in terms of what women may not do and where
they may not go and who they may not be. As Julia Leslie writes
about listening to women's own evaluations of their religious experience, "It is the small deviations from the norm which may be
crucial, perhaps the way the apparently negative is transformed
into something positive and powerful."[26]

   Carmody's story tells of the positive interpretation of a nega-
tively labeled female ritual. Julie Marcus speaks similarly of Turk-

ish Muslim women who place the experience of giving birth in the central position, at the center of being female and of femaleness, not as something unclean or polluted as orthodox Muslim symbolism would suggest.[27] Frédérique Marglin shows that although Hindu women may be considered impure while menstruating and in childbirth, they are nevertheless simultaneously auspicious, "the creators and the maintainers of life, the sources of prosperity, well-being, and pleasure."[28]

In chapter 3, I outlined the original idea of taboo as a state of pollution with extraordinary power. When women are in a state of taboo they are imbued with spirit, *mana*, extraordinary power. They are polluted with power. This means that the body space into which they must retreat so that others may be safe from this potentially overwhelming power provides a new sacred space, and the time of taboo provides a new sacred time for them. Their isolation from the safe, controlled, mediated, constructed forms of religion takes them into a dimension of sacred space and sacred time that is risky, uncontrolled, unmediated, and unconstructed—what I would call a place of wild power.[29]

Although I do not regard it as a new idea, it is probably good to be reminded that the state of taboo or isolation or marginalization of women has the potential to be the center for a woman's religious life. I would add that the communal aspect of women's taboo, which is often lacking from men's taboo experience, affords a time for communal religious experience that may well strengthen an individual woman's religious life.

Of course, not all women may choose or be able to choose to see a positive religious experience within the state of taboo. Patricia Jeffery lived with the women near the shrine of the Muslim Sufi saint Hazrat Nizamuddin Auliya, near Delhi, and noted that during times of fast, some women took pains to conceal their menstrual period so that they could continue with fasts, and secretly got their sisters to do their work so that no one would know.[30] The women were able to get on with the business of practicing their religion by subverting the purity regulations that would otherwise have prevented this. It was clearly more important to them to be able to fast than to submit to the potentially positive taboo state.

Other women, perhaps, may find a heightened sense of religious experience from having had to wait out a taboo state for many years. I wonder if the mainly postmenopausal women who make the pilgrimage to Mecca (*hajj*) after long years of waiting might say that the experience far outweighs any others they have had. Of course, I would also want to ask them to reflect on the kind of spiritual preparation that they might have done in the times of menstrual taboo during all the years leading up to their pilgrimage experience.

You may think that the word "wild" is an odd qualifier to use in relation to the power that women experience in states of taboo and marginality. How is a woman who acknowledges the taboo space (usually somewhere in the domestic space) as her sacred space thereby making contact with wild power and relating to it in a spiritual life? Homes in general hardly seem wild places, although they can be often chaotic. I want to make three points in relation to the term wild: First, I suppose that there are women who have experienced the power of their taboo state as wild at some stage; second, it may well be that some women in taboo state have experienced sacred power in the ordinary moments of relationship and in doing ordinary things like sweeping a house with mindfulness; third, when I speak of wild power, I am speaking of unpredictable power, not necesssarily something that will manifest in wild behavior or make women act wildly. In the taboo or marginal state, women have to deal with a power that is unpredictable and not encompassed by any set of dogmas or theologies.

I also dealt in chapter three with the male religious professional view that women who follow a path of holiness or enlightenment have denied their sexuality or experienced a kind of sex change by choosing a life of virginity. I can also ask celibate women to speak of their own views in this matter. For some, the understanding of themselves as female may be important. Thus a "fully surrendered" woman within the Hindu Brahma Kumari sect might speak about her celibate life as a woman of power in devotion to Shiva—or Shiv Baba, as Brahma Kumari members know him.[31]

The Muslim saint Rabi'a might speak of the offers of marriage she received but refused, of her life among ordinary people as an unmarried woman, of her image of spiritual marriage with her god. She is reported to have said to one of her suitors, Hasan of Basra: "Here existence has ceased, since I have ceased to exist and have passed out of Self. My existence is in Him, and I am altogether His. I am in the shadow of His command. The marriage contract must be asked for from Him, not from me."[32] Her nightly prayer, as she stood on the roof of her house, is reported to have been this: "O my Lord, the stars are shining and the eyes of men are closed, and kings have shut their doors and every lover is alone with his beloved, and here I am alone with Thee."[33]

Centering the Body

In chapter 3, I presented an extensive section on the marginalization of women by the imagery and concepts that religious traditions use about women's bodies and their sexuality. Given the way in which this rhetoric has operated for so long against women, it may be difficult for some women to take their place in center stage to speak about their bodies. Perhaps those who can do so will speak about the isolation of marginalization, which has placed them in another sacred space, a natural sacred space that is the center of religious experience as opposed to a woman's marginal space in the constructed cultic sacred spaces of conventional religious architecture. I have spoken of this to some extent above when attempting to center the concept of taboo.

One of my students, Julie Alderson, captured this idea of the body as sacred space in an image of the total body covering of the Muslim woman (the *chador*) as sacred architecture around the sacred space of the womb for the ritually impure Muslim woman. Some women may find the image of the womb as a center for women's sacred space and religious experience particularly apt, given the fears and prohibitions that relate to that bodily organ in so many of the world's religions. In contrast to such fear and prohibitions, many of the new feminist spiritualities make much of the power of the womb and of the life-stages of women with respect to fertility in the triadic symbol of virgin, mother, and crone. More recently, the triadic symbol has been developed and broadened to include other key archetypes (e.g., in Davis and Leonard).[34] This attempt to reclaim from traditional religion the spiritual significance within the life-stages of women can be very positive and empowering for women.

It may also be that there are available positive images of women's bodies and positive concepts about the power of their sexuality that have received little attention within traditions and that require some research to bring them to general attention. I came across a good example of little known positive images of women's bodies and sexuality within the Christian tradition some years ago while on a short holiday in England. I was taken one day to see three very old Christian churches in Herefordshire, at Kilpeck, Holgate, and Tugford, where there were *sheela-na-gigs*: carvings of little squatting female figures, legs apart, with knees bent and hands passed underneath them to hold open their genitalia. (I was later to learn that many sheelas are found in Ireland and Great Britain, and some also in France).

The sheela on the Norman church at Kilpeck was set up among the corbels with a whole host of other human and animal shapes. Although some of the more sexually explicit carvings with male and female figures had long ago been defaced, the sheela, strikingly, had not been. The sheela at Tugford was badly weathered, and again, she was high up in the chancel wall outside the church. The most striking of all were the two little figures at Tugford, not so much for their carving but because the church had no other artistic adornment besides these two sheelas, and they were inside the church, to the left and right of the south doorway.

The custom of displaying a sheela by the entrance, as at Tugford, seems an old tradition (throughout the Middle Ages and even down to the Renaissance), and there are instances of late settings, where sheelas have been put up by the entrance to a holy well, still in use, or in the wall of an old mill by the entrance where the grain is taken in.

In general, the figures are taken to embody two attitudes, that of sexual display and that of watchfulness, their intention being

primarily to ward off evil and perhaps also to promote fertility.
Anne Ross considers that, in their earliest iconographic form, the
figures may portray the territorial or war goddess in her hag-like
aspect. Her representation has been set into Christian churches—
and her pagan aspect thereby purified—to channel to Christians
her powers of promoting fertility and averting evil in the area over
which she once ruled.[35]

With this example, I conclude the section devoted to the centering of marginal aspects of women's religious experience that
I dealt with in chapter 3 and to the highlighting of some aspects
of women's experience that have been central but unrecognized
as such. In the following section, I focus on women's independent religious life, which might be said to be generally invisible
rather than marginal.

WOMEN'S INDEPENDENT
SPIRITUAL/RELIGIOUS LIFE

It is hard for me to imagine that for centuries and centuries
women have defined themselves or reflected on their experience
only as permanently marginalized persons in relation to the mainstream cultic and social life of the major religions. Within religious traditions, although the male professionals may claim the
right to determine the tradition, the women very often develop
a complementary tradition of their own. However, women's complementary traditions are mostly excluded from discussions about
their role in religions. The same is also true of religious traditions
in a negative sense, of course, as Karma Lekshe Tsomo illustrates
for Buddhism: Official texts speak theoretically about the spiritual equality of men and women, since enlightenment is not understood in gendered terms, yet inequalities exist within the institutionalized forms of this religion in some cultures.[36]

I mentioned briefly in chapter 3 the public pilgrimages of Muslim women to the shrines of saints or holy men. Although often
considered un-Islamic by Muslim clerics, such activity may be central to Muslim women's religious life. Julie Marcus reports that

the shrines are overwhelmingly visited by women.[37] Women at the shrines advise newcomers, consult, pray, and sell objects necessary for the rites.[38] Marcus writes in particular of the shrine tomb of Susuz Dede and describes the making of vows in return for divine help as well as the doing of other activities, such as the distribution of offerings there among the women. It is inclusive activity, building community among women and across class boundaries, a community that "helps to create the open, friendly, welcoming atmosphere that characterises these occasions, despite the incredible bustle."[39] The author describes the shrines as "islands of women's space within the landscape," the place of pilgrimage "out from the household center and its social structures into the liminal world of the shrines in which a set of universal, unifying and transcendental values are reaffirmed as emphatically those of women."[40]

There is a photograph of a woman at a shrine, entitled "At the Sheikh's Stone, Fayyoum Province, Egypt," taken by Winifred Blackman in 1923.[41] In the central focus are two women on the ground, one comforting the other, her arms around her. Graham-Brown comments that it is a sick woman being consoled by another woman. There are a number of men on the edge of the photo simply standing and watching. The picture is a study in intimacy and shared community that surely sums up the significance of the shrines for Muslim women.

Just as the independent rituals or gatherings of women occur on the margins of the official cults of religious traditions, so also do the independent roles that women take tend to be marginal. In many traditions, women have been psychics, mediums, and healers. Such women are found in all the major established religious traditions. When they speak from the center, I may hear about the difficulties they have with their own religious traditions because they are independent professionals, generally labeled as superstitious or linked with magic as opposed to religion. But I also see them standing among the ordinary folk as they speak to me of the needs of ordinary people to solve or alleviate the problems that they face day to day rather than of the bigger issues about salvation and spiritual liberation. In such a situation, the women may actually experience an enhancement of their social position and a freeing up of the social expectations or limitations they normally encounter.[42]

If I acknowledge that women have independent religious lives, is it also true that there is a spiritual identity that is particular to women? Is there an essential difference between women's spiritual experience and men's spiritual experience? I am not talking here about what is sometimes called women's "religiosity"; that is, their religious affiliation, the frequency with which they attend religious ceremonies or festivals, the frequency with which they pray, and so on. There is a great deal of evidence to support the statement that women are more "religious" than men in this regard. I am also not talking about the differences in the types of imagery that women and men use of deity, about the different (stronger) emphasis women might put on the emotional and intuitive aspects of faith, and so on.[43]

Some women certainly feel themselves to have a different spirituality from that of men, whether they judge this in positive or negative terms. Women interviewed by Elizabeth Ozorak were very positive for the most part about women's spirituality, one woman claiming that women feel more deeply and have a greater capacity for caring, for love, and for spirit.[44] Among women interviewed by Deborah Selway, the Muslim woman felt there was not much difference between men's and women's spirituality but went on to say that she found that "there are more males that are spiritually aware than there are females. They have a deeper awareness."[45] The Buddhist woman Tsultrim Allione claims that enlightenment is different for women[46] and that there is a need to incorporate childbearing as part of the path,[47] and the Buddhist woman Karma Lekshe Tsomo claims that "women are equally destined, perhaps especially gifted (judging from the relative numbers of women drawn to religion and the contemplative life), to realize this enlightened mode of being."[48]

Both in this section and in the section on centering with which I began, I have used very positive examples and images about women's religious experience. Of course, in doing that, I do not mean to imply either that all religious experiences of women are positive or that the effect women have as religious leaders or guides is always positive. A case in point is the Shi'ite pilgrimage to the Arabian Sea in 1983 led by the father of Naseem Fatima. Naseem Fatima had had various revelations, mostly in dreams, beginning in 1981. She was also considered to have performed miracles. Eventually, she conducted meetings and began to dominate the life of the village. The community became divided over whether or not she was a genuine mystic, since some of her predictions did not come true. Finally, she was asked in a dream to request the community to plunge into the sea as an expression of their faith. Women and children were placed in six trunks, and Naseem Fatima's father led the people into the sea in the belief that a path would open and lead them into Karbala, the Shi'ite holy city in Iraq. Half of the people died; ten of the sixteen women lost their lives.[49]

Akbar Ahmed reports that Sunni Muslims thought the whole incident was bizarre and insane but that Shi'ite Muslims, having a greater predilection for the supernatural, sacrifice, persecution, death, and martyrdom, found that it "established their superior love for Islam."[50] The story seems important because of Naseem's prominent position in creating a new legend, not only for Shi'ite Muslims, but for Shi'ite women. It also illustrates well how different groups within religious traditions may judge a woman's experience as positive or negative according to their own set of criteria.

CONTEMPORARY STRATEGIES FOR MOVEMENT TO THE CENTER

In the first two sections of this chapter, I have invited women into the center in order to listen and have investigated the idea of women's independent religious life. Women themselves have been following strategies to place themselves in the center also. Especially since the post-World War II period of the twentieth century, women have intentionally joined together in movements of solidarity and concerted effort to critique both the marginaliza-

tion of women in general and their marginalization within religious traitions. Women's movements currently and in the recent
past are having and have had an enormous influence even on the
global scene. This has meant new attempts at finding or forming
religious or spiritual identities and of postulating an authority to
underpin them, reaffirmations of older identities, and criticisms
of the previously assigned identities for women within religious
traditions. It should be clear by now that all manner of motivations could be expected to be involved in such an enterprise, the
issue of power being one of them.

   In the subsections that follow, I will outline just a few of the
possible strategies that women are following. In a sense, all of
them are concerned with dissolving or collapsing boundaries, real
or imagined, and the movement takes place on a number of
planes—from present to past and back again; outward from particular traditions to engage other traditions; inward to engage aspects of a single tradition or, even further, to engage the total
group of those who call themselves women; and finally, outward
again beyond traditions to collapse the boundaries between public and private in order to engage the entire political community.

Back to the Beginning

Current strategies of centering often have some aspect of searching for origins, for the "purity" or "pure original core" of a particular religious tradition, for the *real* history of a religious tradition, for what *real* spirituality is.

EARLIEST IS BEST. Many women writers within religious traditions
look back to a kind of golden age for women members in the very
earliest days of the history of the tradition. In the initial stages of
the foundation of a tradition, the religious and social perspectives
on women members often show considerable differences. Founding figures like the Buddha or Jesus, though still influenced by
their respective cultures, nevertheless show some opposition to
the prevailing negative social norms in their treatment of women.

   It is generally in the second generation of the tradition that the impetus for members to settle down to life in the everyday world requires taking on the usual patterns of thought and custom that prevail in the particular sociocultural setting and adapting the vision of the founder to that particular setting by a process of reinterpretation aimed at social integration. Even in a tradition like Buddhism, where the doctrine concerning the key goal of enlightenment is quite clearly nongendered, there is nevertheless opposition after the death of the Buddha to the inclusion of women in the ranks of religious professionals or ascetics. Nancy Schuster reports that by the late sixth century the monks were well in control and the previous high regard for nuns was a thing of the past.[51]

There seems to be some question, however, about the Buddha's attitude himself to women's inclusion in the community of religious professionals (*sangha*). Traditions after his death portray him as reluctant to allow women into the sangha. There is a text in which Ananda asks the Buddha why women do not take part in public office, and he replies that they are uncontrolled, envious, and weak in wisdom: "That is the reason . . . why womenfolk do not sit in a court of justice, do not embark on business, do not reach the essence of the deed."[52] Some writers conclude that the Buddha thought lay life was more appropriate for women and that "the ideal Buddhist man was always closer to Buddhahood than the ideal Buddhist woman."[53] On the other hand, Karma Lekshe Tsomo says that the Buddha was reluctant to admit women into the sangha because of "the prevailing social conditions" rather than "women's potential for enlightenment."[54]

The problem with early traditions about women who were disciples or supporters of religious founders is that it is often hard to tell from subsequent tradition what the actual situation had been. Thus, the texts and oral traditions in particular have to be scrutinized to some extent to find earlier layers of tradition that might give us a picture of what the case might have been. As with the Buddha, there also appears to have been some ambivalence in the portrayal of Jesus' treatment of women as well. Certainly, women were counted among his early disciples and followers, but he himself seemed not to have made any criticism of the structures that oppressed women at that time—unless that criticism was implicit in his actions.

Muslim historians argue that Muhammad, too, was a liberal founder figure in his treatment of women. They point to a previous lack of rights of Arabian women to inheritance and property, the practice of female infanticide, unregulated polygamy, and pervasive prostitution. However, Leila Ahmed presents a long and provocative challenge to this commonly held view that Islam improved the status of women. She contrasts the freedoms of pre-Islamic women like Muhammad's first wife, Khadija, with the restrictions of Islamic women. For most of her life Khadija must be understood as a *jahiliyya* (pre-Islamic) woman.[55] Given Khadija's clear financial independence as a Meccan trader, the common view that women could not inherit or own property before Islam is erroneous. Ahmed goes on to document that divorce could be initiated by both men and women, that there were uxorilocal matrilineal marriage practices (exemplified in Muhammad's mother's own case), and that women as well as men might have more than one spouse, such that polygamy and polyandry were practiced.[56] In contrast to these practices where women had some freedom and agency, Muhammad instituted one form of marriage based on male rights.[57] Ahmed concludes that one of Muhammad's prime objectives was "the absolute empowerment of men in relation to women in all matters relating to sexuality and offspring and the disempowerment of women. . . ."[58]

"PUREST" IS BEST. Some arguments about returning to the purity of the origins of a tradition focus on practices or customs that are now part of the tradition but that go back to a time before the founder or founding group. Such practices or customs are thought to be foreign to the tradition, and a case is often made that they should not be included in contemporary practice. Fatima Mernissi argues, for example, that attitudes to menstruation and childbirth within Islam originated in pre-Islamic Judaism and, like so many other Muslim attitudes to women, are not Islamic at all but come from the period of "ignorance" (*jahiliyya*) prior to the rise of Islam.[59] Thus, Mernissi is arguing that the *real* Islam should not include oppressive elements from pre-Islamic times. These arguments of Mernissi complement those which suggest that Islam brought improvements to women's plight in Arabian society.

BACK TO THE GODDESS/THE FEMININE. I spoke in chapter 2 of women defining religion/spirituality and of the move some women have made to return to pagan or goddess religions in the process of redefining spirituality or religion.[60] Apart from the key symbol of the Goddess, many women's groups focus on redefining the spiritual aspects of a woman's life-stages. Feminine imagery is realigned with the sacred or the goddess, and a link is made in spiritualities between the earth, with its fecundity and life, and women, with their sexuality and life.

Though earlier scholarship and belief that presented a picture of pure origins—of goddess-centered and peaceful matriarchal societies before their overthrow by patriarchal societies based in the cult of the warrior—have been severely criticized,[61] women continue to reimagine the goddess and to set the feminine at the center of their spiritualities. Women are interested in goddesses in all their symbolic aspects of the sacred feminine—though as Jo Ann Hackett notes, they seem most interested in fertility aspects.[62] There is a creative reimagining both of the goddesses of the old myths and of the old rituals where something is known of them from ancient sources. As Mircea Eliade writes, the burning of the sanctuary at Eleusis and the suppression of the mysteries celebrating the myth of Demeter and Persephone marked the *official* end of paganism—not its disappearance, but merely its occultation.[63]

However, not all of the goddesses in whom women are currently finding meaning and direction for their spiritual paths are those of ancient times. The press, the Internet, and especially the women's magazines offer stories of a fascinating constellation of glamorous, rich, and beautiful stars who live an extraordinary life that most people only dream of. I would suggest that they are the new heavenly council. The greatest of them in recent history was Diana, Princess of Wales, the new goddess for the ordinary

woman, hailed as an icon of postfeminism and new traditional-
ism. She was glamorous and beautiful, a presence and savior for
the poor and disadvantaged, but—above all—she provided the
impetus people need to find meaning within struggle and human
frailty and loneliness, side by side with the seeming perfection of
glamor, beauty and riches.

BACK TO THE BODY, BACK TO THE EARTH—THERE IS NOTHING PROFANE.
Many looking for a new spiritual identity are rediscovering old
streams of spirituality within traditions and finding new possibilities that offer an integrated vision of body and spirit, of spirit
and the natural world. It is a vision that is not limited to the human, but rather celebrates all—humans, animals, plant life, bac-
teria, minerals—that have a part in one great living breathing
body (sometimes represented by the symbol of the ancient Greek
earth goddess, Gaia), the biotic community, where nothing is profane but, rather, all is sacred. Some of those espousing this spiritual vision speak of themselves as "ecofeminists."[64] For them, the
feminist agenda, which aimed at the liberation of human beings
from the oppressive structures and policies of patriarchy, has been
broadened to include a concern and action for the liberation of
all that lives and suffers under such oppression. Much of the writing, though acknowledging the damage done to the biotic community by abusive ecological and economic policies and practices,
shows a tendency toward belief in a kind of end-time paradise or
utopia, which echoes the earlier writings of traditions like Judaism
with its vision of an end state in which the entire earth experiences a return to paradise. In such a paradise, the spiritual liberation of human beings is indissolubly linked to the liberation
of all that lives.

Where nothing is profane, all activity and all times and places
are opportunities for spiritual growth. As Hannah Ward writes,
"It matters how I cook, what I eat, how much sleep I get. I'm quite
convinced those things contribute more to the state of my soul
than how many times a week I fail to get to morning prayer or
whether or not I go to church on Sunday morning."[65] These ideas
complement earlier material in this chapter on women in the do-

mestic arena whose spirituality centers on the home and private spaces away from the official public cult of religious traditions.

Weaving and Networking

In the previous section, I spoke of the integrated vision of body and spirit, of nature and spirit, that many women espouse in a new or reimagined spirituality. Such a vision of integrated life feeds from and supports practical activity on a variety of levels. Such activity is not new. Women have always been concerned for networking, as I have shown with examples such as the gathering together of Muslim women of different class and economic levels at the tombs of the saints. And a networking of equals is implied in the concept of auspiciousness applied to women in Hinduism, an auspiciousness that—despite Hinduism—knows no caste distinctions.[66] However, many women now have the advantage of greater mobility or opportunity of communication with others, so such activity can be more intentionally organized even on the global scene. International meetings of women from isolated and economically deprived indigenous communities, either in person or via such means as the Internet, constitute merely one sign of the new movement. Women are beginning to realize the value of virtual religious spaces on the Internet for a variety of reasons. Women's domestic space is so often restricted space, and yet a woman is also expected to broaden even those restricted boundaries of her space to include perhaps the needs of children and a partner. Where women feel themselves limited in domestic spaces, the Internet may offer greater possibilities for conversation and spiritual community.

At the end of chapter 3, I used an image of women on the margins of traditions turning outward to speak with other women on other margins. The dialogue may be about a variety of issues— ideas, methodologies, spiritualities, or social/ecological concerns—or may take the form of shared liturgies or spiritual activity.

Within the academic arena, women scholars are speaking with others across traditions as they might not have done previously.

The Muslim scholar Amina Wadud-Muhsin, for example, in her attempt to offer a meaningful way of living to Muslim women by a reading of the Qur'an, investigates a number of ways in which other women are doing interpretation of sacred texts now and the way in which others have done interpretation in the past. This makes clear that there are similarities across traditions now for those who wish to remain believers and to find justification and liberation within the authoritative scriptures. Her work weds Western interpretive approaches to Christian or Jewish scriptures with a believer's attitude to the Qur'an.

There is a similar sense of networking in the Buddhist Tsultrim Allione's work. In the introduction to *Women of Wisdom*, Allione quotes Carol Christ, Starhawk, Judith Plaskow, and others as voices of authority in a discussion about the need to have women's stories as examples for other women.[67] Karma Lekshe Tsomo writes of her own attempt to find a new way for women monastics and ascetical wanderers in her aim of synthesizing a multitude of views, including those from other traditions. In a most interesting vignette, she describes the well-read books on her window sill, where *Monastic Discipline for Buddhist Nuns* sits side by side with Mary Daly's *Gyn/Ecology*.[68]

Mary Hunt offers the new spiritual image of "Many Women" ("the image of divine community in which we participate"), an image that expresses most appropriately this activity of networking:

> Many Women are found in women's spaces, at music festivals and conferences, among friends at holiday times, at international gatherings. Women from all over the globe join in sustained conversation, enjoyment, dancing and the building of friendships.[69]

The movement across boundaries to find a new identity also occurs within traditions. Women are beginning to look at aspects of their own tradition that may have been virtually invisible to them previously, either because there was little emphasis on writings outside of the authoritative scriptures or because labels of heterodoxy were imposed on such material. Thus, Christian women scholars are finding new inspiration, for example, in Gnostic texts like *Pistis Sophia*, in which Mary Magdalene is given great prominence, or in texts like *Thunder, Perfect Mind*, with its enigmatic hymn to the feminine.

You may recall that in chapter 2, among the questions I posed as part of the hermeneutical process, I included the following:

- Who am I in relation to the term *woman* as I listen to these women?
- How do I allow my mind to be broad enough to hear all of the possibilities for the women who tell their stories and to have other understandings of the term *woman*?

Movement across boundaries in the search for new spiritual identity has also opened up new networking possibilities within the group of those who call themselves women. Lesbian women, especially, are having much more influence and are offering new perspectives that take the religious questions even further than previously. If a view from the margins is sometimes clearer, then the view that lesbian women have had, being much more marginalized generally than heterosexual women in contemporary societies, may provide even greater challenges and a more radical critique than before within the search by women for spiritual identity.

Dissolving the Public-Private/Heaven-Earth Binarisms

I have already outlined how women's social and religious roles and activities have, in general, been relegated to the domestic or private spheres. The movement to new spiritual identities that incorporate a concern for global issues goes hand in hand with a new political spiritual activism. Thus, those involved in ecofeminist spiritual paths inevitably find themselves engaged in political activity, such as peace, social justice, and green movements.

There is, in general, a trend currently to balance concern for following the more esoteric forms of individual or communal spiritual paths with more social concerns, with a focus on this world rather than on a spiritual or invisible one that is above, or of more significance than, this world. Of course, such a movement could also be seen as a kind of backlash from women against those tactics by religious traditions in which spiritual or otherworldly (i.e., antibody, antisexuality) concepts have been used to oppress them.

Thus, political and social criticism and action are seen as ways of being spiritual or growing spiritually—whether women engage in that action in their local area or across cultural and national boundaries. Current writing on women in particular religious traditions may, in fact, not even make reference to the more traditional aspects of being "religious." Barbara Callaway and Lucy Creevey's book on Muslim women in West Africa, for example, has a section devoted to religion in which they focus on women's involvement and levels of authority within the major Muslim brotherhoods in northern Nigeria and in Senegal rather than on their religious participation per se.[70] I will take up this point again in the following chapter.

CONCLUSION

In this chapter, I have outlined techniques for inviting or drawing women out of the margins to speak from center stage and some strategies by which contemporary women are centering the margins. I should make clear that the idea of moving women's experience to the center does not imply that I am placing others on the margins in their stead—this would simply be to follow the same power games (albeit in reverse agency) already at work in societies and religious traditions. The primary motivation for inviting women to the center is that I might be better able to see or hear them speak of their experiences and might accept and treasure their experiences as real and valid religious experience.

There is one final important question that I need to ask. If I am inviting women from the margins to the center, where am I standing to do that? Letty Russell speaks of the movement from center to margin and vice versa, of those who are marginalized choosing to stand there and work or perhaps move to the center in order to be able to "talk back," of those who are at the center of power and influence choosing the margin to stand in solidarity with those who are oppressed there.[71] I see in a particular way because of where I am standing to look. If I am approaching the study of women's religious experience from a place within the academic community, I cannot presume to stand outside either the center or margin in order to do that. I must place myself both academically and personally somewhere in relation to these positions, and perhaps I need to consider changing that position frequently to gain greater understanding. As Russell comments, "The movement from center to margin and margin to center is a constant motion in both directions as we ask why anyone ought to be on the margin."[72]

Notes

1. The image of movement from margin to center is not new; see, e.g., bell hooks, *Feminist Theory: From Margin to Center* (Boston: South End Press, 1984).

2. See the summary in Elizabeth Puttick, *Women in New Religions: In Search of Community, Sexuality and Spiritual Power* (Basingstoke, U.K.: Macmillan, 1997), pp. 175–95. Puttick deals with the three major categories of women leaders: in movements founded by men (pp. 177–83); in movements cofounded by women and men (pp. 183–85); and in movements founded and led by women (pp.185–92).

3. Youngsook Kim Harvey, *Six Korean Women: The Socialization of Shamans* (St. Paul, Minn.: West Publishing, 1979), pp. 1, 3–4.

4. Victoria Bernal, "Gender, Culture, and Capitalism: Women and the Remaking of Islamic 'Tradition' in a Sudanese Village," *Comparative Studies in Society and History*, vol. 36 (1994), p. 58.

5. Donald K. Swearer, *The Buddhist World of Southeast Asia* (Albany: State University of New York Press, 1995), p. 52.

6. Fatima Mernissi, *Women and Islam: An Historical and Theological Enquiry*, tr. Mary Jo Lakeland (Oxford: Basil Blackwell, 1991), pp. 180–82. Mernissi also reports that Saudi women are not allowed to drive. As I was finishing the final draft of this manuscript in December 1998, I heard a news report that Saudi women were now able to learn to drive, if their husbands gave them permission to do so.

7. Barbara Callaway and Lucy Creevey, *The Heritage of Islam: Women, Religion, and Politics in West Africa* (Boulder, Colo.: Lynne Rienner, 1994), p. 3.

8. Sarah Graham-Brown, *Images of Women: The Portrayal of Women in Photography of the Middle East 1860–1950* (New York: Columbia University Press, 1988), p. 212.

9. See, for example, the outline of lives and sayings of exceptional women in Anne Bancroft, *Weavers of Wisdom: Women of the Twentieth Century* (London: Arkana, 1989), and Anne Bancroft, *Women in Search of the Sacred* (London: Arkana, 1996).

10. See June McDaniel, "A Holy Woman of Calcutta," in Donald S. Lopez Jr., ed., *Religions of India in Practice* (Princeton, N.J.: Princeton University Press, 1995), p. 418.

11. Mary Condren, *The Serpent and the Goddess: Women, Religion, and Power in Celtic Ireland* (San Francisco: Harper & Row, 1989), p. 76.

12. For details about the lives of the Hindu women, see David Kinsley, "Devotion as an Alternative to Marriage in the Lives of Some Hindu Women Devotees," *Journal of Asian and African Studies*, vol. 15 (1980), pp. 83–93. It is interesting that women react to these saints differently— Lindsey Harland ("Abandoning Shame: Mira and the Margins of Marriage," in Lindsey Harland and Paul B. Courtright, eds., *From the Margins of Hindu Marriage: Essays on Gender, Religion, and Culture*, New York: Oxford University Press, 1995, p. 206), speaks of Mira Bai and the way in which some Rajput women say that she was above custom, whereas others say that she should have worshiped her husband and not Krishna.

13. Karma Lekshe Tsomo, ed., *Sakyadhita: Daughters of the Buddha* (Ithaca, N.Y.: Snow Lion Publications, 1988), p. 21.

14. Roshi Philip Kapleau, *Awakening to Zen: The Teachings of Roshi Philip Kapleau* (Sydney: Bantam Books, 1997), pp. 142–44.

15. Fatima Mernissi, *The Veil and the Male Elite: A Feminist Interpretation of Women's Rights in Islam* (Reading, Mass.: Addison-Wesley, 1991), pp. 113–14.

16. Itumeleng Mosala, "The Implications of the Text of Esther for African Women's Struggle for Liberation in South Africa," *Semeia*, vol. 59 (1992), p. 136.

17. Amina Wadud-Muhsin, *Qur'an and Woman* (Kuala Lumpur: Penerbit Fajar Bakti, 1992), p. vi.

18. See C. J. Fuller, *The Camphor Flame: Popular Hinduism in Society in India* (Princeton, NJ: Princeton University Press, 1992), p. 63.

19. Roshi Philip Kapleau, ed., *The Three Pillars of Zen: Teaching, Practice, and Enlightenment* (Boston: Beacon Press, 1967), pp. 239–45.

20. Julie Marcus, *A World of Difference: Islam and Gender Hierarchy in*

Turkey (St. Leonards, NSW: Allen & Unwin, 1992), pp. 126–29; and Shibani Roy, *The Status of Muslim Women in North India* (Delhi: B.R. Publishing, 1979), pp. 111–12.

21. Cynthia Ann Humes, "The Goddess of the Vidhyas in Banaras," in Bradley R. Hertel and Cynthia Ann Humes, eds., *Living Banaras: Hindu Religion in Cultural Context* (Albany: State University of New York Press, 1993), pp. 196–200.

22. Manisha Roy, *Bengali Women* (Chicago: University of Chicago Press, 1975), pp. 138–45, 168–70.

23. Madeleine Tress, "Halakha, Zionism, and Gender: The Case of Gush Emunim," in Valentine M. Moghadam, ed., *Identity Politics and Women: Cultural Reassertions and Feminisms in International Perspective* (Boulder, Colo.: Westview Press, 1994), pp. 308–9.

24. Bonnie J. Miller-McLemore, *Also a Mother: Work and Family as Theological Dilemma* (Nashville, Tenn.: Abingdon, 1994), p. 84.

25. Denise Lardner Carmody, *Women and World Religions*, 2nd ed. (Englewood Cliffs, N.J.: Prentice-Hall, 1989), pp. 151–52.

26. I. Julia Leslie, *Roles and Rituals for Hindu Women* (London: Pinter, 1991), p. 3.

27. Marcus, *World of Difference*, p. 124.

28. Frédérique Apffel Marglin, "Female Sexuality in the Hindu World," in Clarissa W. Atkinson et al., eds., *Immaculate and Powerful: The Female in Sacred Image and Social Reality* (Wellingborough, U.K.: Crucible, 1987), p. 40; and *Wives of the God-King: The Rituals of the Devadasis of Puri* (New York: Oxford University Press, 1985), p. 299.

29. Mary Daly (*Pure Lust: Elemental Feminist Philosophy*, London: Women's Press, 1984) also speaks of the wild nature of taboo in relation to women, in that taboo harnesses "our own Elemental powers" (p. 249), but she treats the concept slightly differently in that the wildness is also related to breaking taboo: "Since Wild, Natural Women are Taboo-Breakers of the millenia, we are Taboo and our transgressions are incalculably courageous, contagious" (p. 244).

30. Patricia Jeffery, *Frogs in a Well: Indian Women in Purdah* (London: Zed Press, 1979), pp. 111–12.

31. Lawrence A. Babb, "Indigenous Feminism in a Modern Hindu Sect," in Rehana Ghadially, ed., *Women in Indian Society: A Reader* (New Delhi: Sage Publications, 1988), pp. 278–81.

32. Margaret Smith, "Rabi'a the Mystic," in Elizabeth Warnock Fernea and Basima Qattan Bezirgan, eds., *Middle Eastern Women Speak*, excerpted from Margaret Smith's *Rabi'a the Mystic and Her Fellow-Saints in*

Islam (Cambridge: Cambridge University Press, 1928) (Austin: University of Texas Press, 1977), p. 45.

33. Smith, "Rabi'a," p. 55.

34. See Elizabeth Davis and Carol Leonard, *The Women's Wheel of Life: Thirteen Archetypes of Woman at Her Fullest Power* (Rydalmere, NSW: Hodder and Stoughton, 1996).

35. Anne Ross, "The Divine Hag of the Pagan Celts," in Venetia Newall, ed., *The Witch Figure: Folklore Essays by a Group of Scholars in England Honouring the 75th Birthday of Katharine M. Briggs* (London: Routledge & Kegan Paul, 1973), pp. 148–49.

36. Tsomo, *Sakyadhita*, p. 25.

37. Marcus, *World of Difference*, pp. 130–34.

38. Marcus, *World of Difference*, p. 132.

39. Marcus, *World of Difference*, p. 132.

40. Marcus, *World of Difference*, p. 134.

41. Graham-Brown, *Images of Women*, p. 90.

42. See, e.g., the study of shamanism/spirit possession among the Muslim women in Soheir A. Morsy, "Sex Differences and Folk Illness in an Egyptian Village," in Lois Beck and Nikki Keddie, eds., *Women in the Muslim World* (Cambridge, Mass.: Harvard University Press, 1978), pp. 599–616.

43. See the summaries in Elizabeth Weiss Ozorak, "The Power, but Not the Glory: How Women Empower Themselves Through Religion," *Journal for the Scientific Study of Religion*, vol. 35 (1996), passim.

44. Ozorak, "Power," pp. 25–26.

45. Deborah Selway, *Women of Spirit: Contemporary Religious Leaders in Australia* (Melbourne: Longman, 1995), p. 118.

46. Tsultrim Allione, *Women of Wisdom* (London: Arkana, 1986), p. 16.

47. Allione, *Women*, pp. 18–19.

48. Tsomo, *Sakyadhita*, p. 19.

49. Akbar S. Ahmed, *Pakistan Society: Islam, Ethnicity and Leadership in South Asia* (Oxford: Oxford University Press, 1986), pp. 46–68.

50. Ahmed, *Pakistan Society*, p. 65.

51. Nancy Schuster, "Striking a Balance: Women and Images of Women in Early Chinese Buddhism," in Haddad and Findly, *Women*, p. 103.

52. Nirmala S. Salgado, "Equality and Inequality in Hinduism and Buddhism," in R. Siriwardena, ed., *Equality and the Religious Traditions of Asia* (London: Pinter, 1987), p. 62.

53. Salgado, *Equality*, p. 64.

54. Tsomo, *Sakyadhita*, p. 22.

55. Leila Ahmed, "Women and the Advent of Islam," *Signs: Journal of Women in Culture and Society*, vol. 11 (1986), p. 665.

56. Ahmed, "Women," pp. 668–69.

57. Ahmed, "Women," p. 670.

58. Ahmed, "Women," p. 678.

59. Mernissi, *The Veil*, p. 73.

60. For helpful summaries of the recent history of interest in goddess religion/imagery, see Mary Jo Weaver, "Who Is the Goddess and Where Does She Get Us," *Journal of Feminist Studies in Religion*, vol. 5 (1989), pp. 50–58, and Puttick, *Women*, pp. 196–231.

61. See the summary of the debate in Weaver, "Goddess," pp. 56–58.

62. Jo Ann Hackett, "Can a Sexist Model Liberate Us? Ancient Near Eastern 'Fertility' Goddesses," *Journal of Feminist Studies in Religion*, vol. 5 (1989), pp. 67–68.

63. Mircea Eliade, *A History of Religious Ideas. Vol. 1: From the Stone Age to the Eleusinian Mysteries* (Chicago: University of Chicago Press, 1978), p. 301.

64. For a very helpful outline of the connections between deep ecology, feminism, and ecofeminism, see Rosemary Radford Ruether, *Gaia and God: An Ecofeminist Theology of Earth Healing* (New York: HarperSan Francisco, 1992), p. 2.

65. Hannah Ward, "The Lion in the Marble: Choosing Celibacy as a Nun," in Linda Hurcombe, ed., *Sex and God: Some Varieties of Women's Religious Experience* (New York: Routledge & Kegan Paul, 1987), p. 84.

66. As Marglin (*Wives*, p. 300) writes:

> The principle of the auspicious and the inauspicious is nonhierarchical. Women in that perspective are all of one kind, like the earth. Their blessings are given in the same measure, regardless of their caste.

67. Allione, *Women*, pp. 1–4.

68. Tsomo, *Sakyadhita*, p. 13.

69. Mary E. Hunt, "Friends in Deed," in Hurcombe, *Sex and God*, p. 53.

70. Callaway and Creevey, *Heritage*, pp. 41–53.

71. Letty M. Russell, *Church in the Round: Feminist Interpretation of the Church* (Louisville, Ky.: Westminster/John Knox Press, 1993), p. 26.

72. Russell, *Church in the Round*, p. 27.

5

A Chorus of
Many Voices

—⚭—

I have set out the argument or line of thinking in each preceding chapter in a fairly straightforward and simple manner. I have not paused very often in that process to speak of the difficulties or ambiguities involved in some of the positions that have been advocated, although I have occasionally warned of, or signaled, the kinds of subtlety that would make a difference to the activity of listening or to the method. In all of this, I have advocated a certain line that may have appeared simpler than it actually is. Perhaps this is a good idea in the beginning of such study, knowing that with more reading and study and listening the student of women's religious experience who is convinced of, and practices, the openness necessary for honest dialogue will hopefully become more and more aware of the complexities and subtleties involved in the study.

While I have dealt with the material of women's religious experience, and have noted the remarks and opinions of other scholars here and there, I have made little reference, except in the introduction, to the differences of opinion among scholars themselves and between scholars and those who would not categorize themselves as scholars but nevertheless have written about women's religious experience or have expressed their opinions in some other way. In this final chapter, then, I want to speak about some of these differences of opinion as well as to revisit some of the issues about the study that I have raised in earlier chapters.

MANY VOICES: DIFFERENCE AND DIALOGUE

The aspect of different viewpoints and opinions held by women in the study or analysis of women's religious experience—what I have characterized as a "chorus of many voices" and what Kim Knott calls "polyvocality"[1]—is one of the most difficult aspects I see in doing such study at the moment. Within the concerted effort in the recent past to study and analyze women's religious experience within all the world's religions, there has been a lively (and unfortunately sometimes acrimonious) debate over matters of method and interpretation among women of different races, women of different cultures, women of different religious traditions, women of different intellectual training, and so on.

Philosophical/Social Differences: "Equal but Different"

One of the most contentious philosophical differences among scholars is the "equal but different" issue. This issue is often seen as dividing "Western feminists" from most of the rest of the scholars working on women's issues in general or women's religious experience in particular, but one must be wary of such a limited division and categorization. As I shall point out in the second section below on political differences, "Western" may well be a negative label applied by a religious tradition or political system to all unorthodox or liberal ideas and practices, even where non-Western women might be proposing such things. One must also

be careful of the lines of division in the argument, since the issue is presented as a matter of equality or difference between men
and women, but is often debated in terms of individualism versus community. In this way it is related to the emphasis that some
feminists place on their liberation activity within and for family
and kin.[2]

Patricia Higgins outlines the issue of "equal but different" in
relation to Islam, proposing that Western feminists generally consider difference to result in inequality, whereas Muslim feminists
stress male and female distinctiveness and the desirability of separate spheres of activity for both, which—so they argue—can result in a just, equitable, and harmonious Muslim society, where
individual interests do not take precedence over family or community interests.[3] One consequence of this, as Fatima Mernissi
points out, is that a Muslim woman who considers that she is not
equal and chooses to rebel against her position is thereby re-
belling against the *umma*, the entire community of Islam.[4]

The newly orthodox women in American Judaism whom Debra Renee Kaufmann interviewed appear to think in much the
same way. They do not challenge the patriarchal system that supports and informs their religious tradition, but rather they celebrate feminine difference. They look to enhance the status of
women through communal recognition of the importance of fe-
male-linked practices and symbols within the boundaries of their
religion and social structure, which they consider to give them a
clear set of moral values.[5]

Karma Lekshe Tsomo, too, cautions against applying to Buddhism the ideals of Western feminism about equality. For Tsomo,
the quest for ordination of Buddhist women is not a quest for
equal rights by these women but a quest to be free from the cycle of rebirth (*samsara*).[6] She feels that the important thing for
Buddhist women is not for them to look for equal rights but rather
for them to become independent in their religious lives so that
they do not rely on the facilities provided by monks. Sex discrimination is an ego concern, a mistaken perception, and not
important in the search for enlightenment.[7]

Political Differences: Western Versus non-Western

The early critical feminist study of women's religious experience in the twentieth century was carried out for the most part by European and North American Christian and Jewish feminist scholars. Many of the Christian scholars were subsequently criticized for their Eurocentric and colonialist standpoints, among other things.[8] Like their imperialist predecessors, they were said to be taking a paternalistic attitude toward improving women's lot in non-Western countries and setting a Western white woman's agenda as normative for women's movements worldwide.[9] I have dealt with some problems related to this issue in the introduction.

The mere fact that these early scholars were Western also provided, and continues to provide, an opportunity for political point scoring by non-Western writers. Gender associated with religious and cultural practice has become an important symbol for anti-Western and antimodern political strategies in some countries.[10]

Valentine Moghadam gives a very useful overview of some of these movements currently, their activity characterized as "identity politics"—"discourses and movements organized around questions of religious, ethnic, and national identity" and "political-cultural movements that are making a bid for state power."[11] She identifies the best known religious groups within the movements as Hindu and Muslim—the former in South Asia, the latter in the Middle East and North Africa as well as South Asia—who follow the general trend toward preoccupation with gender and the control of women. She also makes reference to the existence, in the United States, of Jewish orthodox revival groups that constitute another stream within this movement, though these focus on the spiritual rather than the secular world.[12]

In chapter 4, I wrote of the growing emphasis upon political and social criticism and action as a way for women to be spiritual or grow spiritually. How am I to deal with material on women's religious experience that appears to be more political than religious? When the return to traditional religious values is more a political movement than a religious one, does politicized religion cease to be religion and become, in effect, a secular ideology pure

and simple? Can I even think of drawing a line between the political and the religious when, particularly in Hinduism and Islam, woman's nature (and, consequently, spiritual capacity and
religious position) has been determined by those same texts and
passages that determine the structure of society?

Two examples from Islam will serve to illustrate the difficulty.
First, when I listen to the voices of the Iranian-based Marxist group
Emancipation of Women speaking about the various groups of
women in that country who supported veiling in the early 1980s,[13]
the analysis is political and economic rather than having anything
to do with religious status or identification with Fatima, the daughter of Muhammad, as exhorted by Khomeini and others.

Second, Leila Ahmed discusses the work of the early twentieth-
century activist Zeinab al-Ghazali, who claimed to be an Islamic
revivalist focusing on the liberation of women and who founded
the Muslim Women's Association, which helped women study Islam and implemented welfare activites for orphans, the poor, and
the unemployed, while still claiming that women's most important role was motherhood.[14] Ahmed notes that even though al-
Ghazali is presented as a religious revolutionary, she seems to have
had no spiritual commitment to Islam, thereby prompting Ahmed
to comment that, for al-Ghazali, "Islam figures as a path to empowerment, to glory, to a properly regulated society—but not as
a spiritual path."[15]

In coming to some conclusion myself about how to approach
this difficulty of politicized religion or religious politics, I attempted to listen to women involved closer to the phenomenon.
As you might expect, there was no consensus. Let me give the last
word to one Muslim woman who has positive views and two Hindu
women who have negative views on the mix of politics and religion.

In her book *Nine Parts of Desire*, Geraldine Brooks writes of the
gradual rise of more conservative attitudes in Islam, partly from
women. These conservative attitudes may find an outcome in practices that appear to be religious. In speaking with a woman called
Sahar who had made the choice to return to the practice of veiling, Brooks looks at the political nature of that choice. Sahar re-

sponded to Brooks' inquiry as to the reasons for her choice by repeating "the slogan of Islamic Jihad and the Muslim Brotherhood: 'Islam Is the Answer.' "[16]

Clearly, Sahar sees a strong connection between a choice that might be regarded as religious and a commitment to a political movement with strong religious overtones. By contrast, two Hindu women speak in negative terms of the same kind of political movements in India, which conflate politics, religion, and old traditions in new packaging to suit the new politics of nationalist fundamentalist Hindus. John Hawley introduces the feminists Madhu Kishwar and Ruth Vanita, publishers of the magazine *Manushi*, who consider the kind of religion involved in such political movements to be "phoney religion," merely "politics in a very thin disguise" presented as religion and thereby constituting a mystification of religion "that serves the cause of oppressing women."[17]

Differences of Belief and Praxis: Orthodox/Traditional Versus Nonorthodox/Nontraditional

Apart from the first examples of different standpoints of a political and philosophical nature, there are a variety of standpoints about the practical outcome of ideological views. In relation to traditional and nontraditional practice, for example, Brooks describes Muslim women scholars who live a traditional life (i.e., veiled in some way) and who have a little influence on other Muslims, while a feminist such as Mernissi, even though a good scholar, has less credibility because she does not go veiled.[18]

Orthodoxy in relation to method is also a bone of contention among women scholars. I have already dealt in chapter 3 with the marginalization of women by the text-based view of orthodoxy held by academics and by male religious professionals. Feminist scholars of sacred texts, whether they be Christian or Jewish or Muslim, can be guilty of the same limited view of their traditions if they link the status and liberation of women exclusively with scripture and its interpretation. This is to say nothing of the differences of opinion expressed by the text critics themselves about the methods by which they interpret.[19]

I have dealt with women's experience in familiar and unfamiliar contexts within the earlier chapters of this book. In some cases, the contexts may have been scarcely recognizable as the same traditions that are presented in textbooks on religion. Such is often the case when dealing with the reality of people's everyday lives rather than some ideal believer's image as presented in textbooks. But there are generally some key practices or symbols within a religious tradition that remain constant, however tangential the actual experience of believers may be to that tradition.

Within recent work by women Buddhist scholars have been some forceful suggestions about the necessity for change in that tradition. Rita Gross has suggested that change may be necessary in what she herself describes as "the beloved heart of Buddhist life"; that is, the Buddhist emphasis on meditation and spiritual disciplines. She questions whether meditation really helps someone to "live well and truthfully" or whether it is simply a creation of patriarchs, used "to control life and distance themselves from others."[20]

In her critique of Tantric Buddhism, June Campbell advocates women reclaiming what is whole in themselves rather than understanding themselves as a symbol to achieve wholeness. She thus undermines the fundamental understanding of Tantric Buddhism, in which male and female are not whole in themselves but only make a whole when joined.[21]

Taking Starhawk as her inspiration—and the idea that all life is wonder and suffering is a part of learning—Tsultrim Allione challenges the fundamental tenet of Buddhism that all experience is suffering or unsatisfactoriness and that one must try to escape from the round of rebirths into the light or nirvana.[22]

The three women are practicing Buddhists who are also committed to the feminist cause. They have proposed changes to Buddhism that seem to attack the very heart of it—to the extent that it would seem to be no longer recognizable as Buddhism. When we attempt to study ideas of this nature, there may be an added dimension to the dialogue. A number of voices may need to be heard, not only those of the women who practice a particular religion but also the dialogue between those women practitioners and the tradition to which they are committed and between the student and the religious tradition as previously understood by the student.

Differences of Belief and Praxis: Academic Versus Nonacademic; Critical Versus Noncritical

Difference may also be found between academics and nonacademics within particular traditions or even across traditions. Two points are worth noting. First, there can be a kind of arrogance, perhaps unintentional, in some academic work as scholars try to "put things right" or show women how oppressed they are or how wrong they are. Perhaps this underlies the frustration that I hear in Chatsumarn Kabilsingh's voice as she speaks of the irritating problem she encountered with Thai Buddhist nuns who were not very interested in changing the situation of the double standard operating both politically and socially against them.[23] Second, it has become rather commonplace, when attending women's conferences or gatherings, to hear much rhetoric, either publicly or behind the scenes, against "the academics" and the analytical nature of their discourse about women's religious experience. Those who make such comments seem generally in favor of a less critical appropriation of symbols or rituals for women's spirituality or a simple experiential approach to understanding women's religious experience. There may also be a perspective that academics have become caught up in the (mostly) male system in which they work and thus cannot be trusted not to be seduced by it.

I understand such rhetoric against arrogance because it can be well founded, and I can understand rhetoric against an unbalanced and exclusively overcritical view of what women are doing as they search for an authentic spirituality or religious tradition. However, I must state my own bias here in favor of a wary approach to all such appropriation of material by women to serve their spiritual or academic purposes. I agree, for example, with Diane Purkiss' sound refutation of the generally incorrect popular (and, in some cases, scholarly) views proposed about early modern European witches[24]; and with Dolores Williams about appropriating uncritically African sources as liberating for women[25];

and with Mary Jo Weaver's criticism, which I noted in chapter 4, of the idea of ancient utopian goddess-centered matriarchal societies.[26]

I need to be wary of attempts to reclaim from traditional religion the spiritual significance of feminine images and symbols that seem to be as much limited by using biology as a basis for doing theology as are the papal pronouncements that make a connection between the female creative womb and a creative God. I have already spoken of this briefly in the introduction. I have to question Karma Lekshe Tsomo when she states that equating spirituality with sexuality (by which she includes gender) is a Western error and that Buddhism sees beyond such an error of conflation,[27] but then goes on in another place to say that women may be especially gifted to realize enlightenment because so many women are drawn to religion and a contemplative life.[28]

The reclaiming or the reimagining of goddess-centered religion or spirituality, with its attendant difficulties, provides a good example to reflect on, since this reclaiming and reimagining is such a powerful movement currently in women's spirituality—and it is also perhaps the most publicly recognized movement.[29] What kinds of difficulties could possibly underlie what appears to be such a positive movement for women from a variety of backgrounds? Let me point to just one difficulty that I see. Many women's spirituality groups that I know of speak quite freely about "the Goddess," a kind of generic figure who embodies some idea about a powerful spiritual life-force immanent in the world. However, they also use in various ways, for reflection or ritual, texts or songs relating to individual ancient goddess figures, such as Isis, Astarte, or Innana.

The use of the generic Goddess, into which all these individual figures of goddesses may be seen to merge, cannot avoid the difficulties associated with use of the individual goddess figures for reflection and ritual. Although there are positive aspects to the individual goddess figures, such as the key role that they play in vegetation myths—as I pointed out in chapter 2—nevertheless they are also frequently victims in the power struggles in myths that mirror the oppressive structures of the societies in which they arose. Goddesses, for the most part, appear in the role of mother

or wife or companion to a god, and the honor they receive is little more than a reflection of the honor given to their male son,
husband, or lover. Their stories are often stories of suffering because of the god to whom they are related: Isis to Osiris, Cybele
to Attis, the Virgin Mary to Jesus. "Goddess" may sound like a
grandiose title but the title may be deceptive, for even goddesses
of the highest status, such as the Greek goddess Hera, the wife of
the most powerful god Zeus, could suffer from domestic violence
on a cosmic scale.

I am not suggesting that women should not use the Goddess,
or some particular individual goddess, as a positive liberating symbol for themselves. I have used these symbols myself. What I do
suggest is that women should not use the symbol unthinkingly—
that they need to understand the possible dangers inherent in
what they are choosing to use. The ancient myths in which these
goddesses appear were most probably written by men and thus
are products of patriarchal cultures, with the very real possibility
that the goddess figures in the myths may be little more than representations of men's fears and fantasies about women played out
on the stage of the cosmos.

In this section, I have outlined simply a variety of differences
in standpoint among women who study and interpret women's
religious experience. I would suggest that we imagine these
women with different opinions, not as antagonists but as people
with views to offer as part of the dialogue in which we wish to im-
merse ourselves as we study women's religious experience. Although I wrote that I see the variety of opinion and method as a
difficult thing, I do not want to lose sight of the fact that difference can also be the most potentially powerful aspect of a dialogue for moving a study forward. The dialectic of opinion and
disagreement can bring about a new appreciation that benefits
all parties engaged in the conversation.

THE CRITICAL INTERPRETING VOICE

I began in chapter 1 with a reflection on the process of interpretation and the way in which this process is a subjective one re-

quiring an outcome in personal and academic judgments. Now
that I have outlined a few of the differences currently found in
studies of women's religious experience, it seems important to reflect again on the process of interpretation and to deal in more
depth here with some of the key issues.[30]

Let me begin again with the simple idea of the subjectivity of
the interpreting process. I doubt that anyone would disagree
much with the opinion that interpreting phenomena is a highly
subjective act, that is, that every interpretation is unique to the
person who interprets. No one else has my history, nor can anyone else stand in my exact position to view the world. All this is
self-evidently true, as is the statement that there are an infinity of
possible interpretations when studying phenomena. Further, the
process of interpretation itself is never completed. It is always
open-ended—a process of apprehending, of being engaged with
the material.

However, this basic point about the subjectivity of the interpreting process is only one aspect of the reality of the situation,
a description of what individual human beings do from one angle. It says nothing of the history of the reception of the material, nothing of the broader context of interpreting beyond the individual. If I limited myself to such a partial description of the
interpreting process, as if it were the full story, I would be taking
a very myopic view of the process. Such a position assumes that
shared human existence is unimportant in the process of interpretation, that the idea of a context for the process within history
and the sense of the community is passé, that there are ultimately
no universal norms about which we might agree that have a bearing on how I interpret and the kinds of judgments I make concerning which interpretations are good or appropriate.

This issue about discriminating among various interpretations
and about the possibility of making a judgment about material
that may be more broadly applied by me than just to my own experience is an important one. It has become fashionable to move
from the idea of the infinite possibilities of interpretation and the
open-ended nature of interpretation to the necessity of the suspension of any judgment, as if that were the logical outcome of
the subjective process of interpretation. In other words, there are

those who would say that because I cannot say anything absolute about the meaning of certain material that I study, I cannot make a judgment about anything. Because there are infinite interpretations, every interpretation must be tolerated. I must be totally open. It seems to me that this creates a kind of amoral vacuum, where all absolutes are gone and no truth remains to which one may commit oneself. There are only shifting sands—nowhere to stand—where nothing may be truly communicated or meaningfully said. What was simply a partial description of how human beings interpret and attempt to understand in an ever-changing world has become a moral paradigm—or, rather, an *amoral* paradigm.

Against the argument for the suspension of moral judgment, I want to assert, as I did in chapter 1, that the logical outcome of the subjective process of interpretation is that I *must* make judgments and that, in fact, it is not possible to suspend them. It is simply not possible to engage any material without making some judgment, without taking some position in relation to it, and this is so because such engagement is a subjective process. The key aspect of the process for the academic interpreter is the attempt to integrate the personal and involuntary reaction to the material studied with the intellectual exercise of consciously applying questions and paradigms and, ultimately, to enter into dialogue with others from a position that is fully acknowledged as both personal and intellectual.[31]

When I make judgments within the process of interpretation, how do I distinguish which ones are good and appropriate from those that are neither?[32] I must reiterate what I have said in chapter 1. Since I do, inevitably, make judgments, it seems to me that I must take my position on material but take it with an openness to dialogue about it and continue reading and listening in order to attempt constantly to discriminate what might be valuable from what might not be. I do not have some absolute truth about the material, but I have an opinion, a reaction. The kind of truth that I have is the acknowledgment that I have had a reaction, that I have taken a position.

The point about dialogue brings me back to the community

(both my own community and other communities) as the context of the activity both of interpreting and of judging. This is the context for making judgment and taking judgment, for judging with a community and against it, for judging among communities of differing cultures and historical settings. This assumes that there is some shared bond between human beings that makes this possible. Yet even if I accept that there is some bond, I am faced with the fact that not all communities will agree on or behave out of common ethical positions—although, as Alan Buchanan suggests, it is highly implausible that there are no basic values shared with past communities and across quite culturally different communities. Such a lack of agreement, however, does not necessarily invalidate judgments made about basic values or human rights. Buchanan uses the example that even if one culture *disagrees* with the position that there exists a basic human right to be free from torture, the conclusion does not *necessarily* follow that no such basic human right exists.[33]

What about judging communities in the past? At the end of my recent article on Isaiah 47 in the Jewish scriptures, I offer a postscript in which I judge that the use of the metaphor of warrior for the Hebrew god Yahweh in the Book of Isaiah is inappropriate or morally questionable when it leads to the possibility of presenting Yahweh as a warrior-rapist.[34] I make this judgment for the Christian community that reads the text today but also suggest that the metaphor was inappropriate even for the community from whom the text originated. When I used this article with one of my classes, many students were uncomfortable about my judging the ancient Hebrew community.

It often seems to me that arguments against judging communities of the past are based on a sort of arrogance that assumes that moral or ethical life is something that has been evolving and that modern communities are thereby much more moral or responsible in this regard. This kind of thinking is similar to that which informs theories about the evolution of religious life from "primitive" animistic beliefs to the "higher" monotheistic systems. Of course, we have more knowledge about certain things in our world that can inform our ethical decision-making, but this does not make us more ethical people than those in the past, nor should we be held as more responsible and open to judgment about our ethical choices than they.

Who makes the decision about what are human rights? Surely this requires some kind of sense of community, of the global community engaged in conversation both across cultures in the present and with communities of the past. I take part in this larger conversation by virtue of my place within the global community, just as, on the smaller scale, I engage in conversation with the phenomena I study by the way that I position and reposition myself in relation to them.[35] As in the global community, so in the microcosmic world of scholarship, the process of making judgments must be informed by an ethics that is pragmatic and practical, in dialogue with those affected by, or included in, my study—as I have suggested in chapter 1. In this way, I learn to distinguish between respect and permissiveness and to avoid the vice of convictionless tolerance.

Within such a dialogue as I suggest, power is present and used in very subtle ways. I have been careful to use the verb "invite" when speaking of moving women's religious experience from the margin to the center in my attempt to study it. It is always possible that some women may not want to move to the center to speak. And I need to avoid the situation where a woman is "put on the spot"—put under the spotlight in the center and made to speak—as if I were some stage critic judging her performance, instead of my being a willing and respectful dialogue partner. There may need to be quite a bit of dialogue first before I even begin to broach an issue about which I have a difference of opinion from the person with whom I wish to speak.

By the very fact that I make a judgment about a certain experience, even if I do not represent it as a universal judgment, I am actually demanding, in a way, that the person with whom I want to be in dialogue should consider my opinion. The other person has to consider at least the possibility that there is something more, another perspective, to be considered and argued for or against or accepted as possible and so on. Conversations can be one-sided or dominated by one of the speakers. I need to prac-

tice self-reflection and self-suspicion within the process, ever striv-
ing to remain aware of Marx's caveat of the hidden relation that
connects ideology to the phenomena of domination.[36] Particularly in cross-cultural dialogue, I must be careful from the very
beginning to take into account where my culture and another's
culture may have been related in the past in unequal positions of
power through a colonial system of oppression.[37]

One-sided or dominating conversations emphasize difference
at the expense of the openness of the partners. Sarah Hoagland
argues that although a dialogue is based in difference, it must not
necessarily follow that the acknowledgment of difference be set
in conflict or antagonism as a way of coming to self-awareness
(contra Hegel)—as if in a paradigm of power caught in the
metaphor of master-slave. She proposes rather a dialogue in which
the partners are "autokoenonous" ("one among many"). In such
a dialogue, the partners have a sense of their personal boundaries, not to limit interaction but to provide the context for moral
activity where one has a part to play in relation to others and to
certain situations.[38]

I have ranged very broadly in this section, but one point seems
to circle again and again through the discussion—the necessity
of situating within the community context both the interpretive
process and the dialogue about the judgments made during that
process. The community should be understood to be as broad as
the community of human beings—or even of the biotic community—and as narrow as the smaller communities within which I
perform my everyday activity. The community is the context for
the activity of interpreting and for the dialogic process of discriminating valuable judgment as well as for that critique that
leads to liberation or to a clearer perception of the issues in a
particular situation. It all sounds rather simple and obvious, but
I think it needs to be said, nonetheless, to counter some of the
distortion being advocated by the excessive subjective relativism
or cultural relativism that has taken hold at present. In the end,
the integrity of the scholar in the activity of interpretation is
bound up with her or his actively critical life within global and
local communities.

CONCLUSION

I set out in this book to offer a hermeneutical process by which to interpret and appreciate women's religious experience. I have organized the more detailed study in chapters 3 and 4 around the image of "center" and "margin." It is a useful image to describe the past and current strategies by which women's religious experience is made and characterized as marginal within world religions and the academy. Ultimately, however, the image of margin and center may not be the most helpful to use of women's religious experience. It is not a positive image for women, since it comes from just one perspective on the position of women in world religions, and perspectives are relevant to where one stands to describe the view. I have also suggested in chapter 4 a reversal of the perspective that sees women's experience as marginal and, instead, an approach to women's experience as central. Finally, it is not a positive model, since the relative positions of center and margin inevitably invite comparison of one position to the other and of the relative power or status given to each.

As I invite women to come to the center to speak, I have said that I am not moving anyone to the margin at the same time, such that the position of the margin is dissolved. Still, if all are in the center, the use of the image "the center" no longer seems appropriate, since there would be no margins to define the center. When I imagine all women and men standing in a place that has no center and no margins, the most appropriate image is that of community. I want to take seriously the work of the ecofeminists and to imagine that the community consists not only of women and men but of all that human beings are related to, beginning with the concept of the biotic community—a network of relationships among all living elements. Such a perspective breaks the arrogance of patriarchal systems of power, which presume that humans have their rightful place at the center of life, that men have their rightful place at the center of all life, and that those with power over others have their rightful place at the center of human life.

Thus, the biotic community works against privileging humans in disproportionate power systems. In this community, by contrast with patriarchal systems, human beings would recognize their place as merely one living species among all living elements, they would come to speak authentically from their place as human beings, and women—as human beings within this biotic community—would not only be empowered to speak, individually and together, of their religious experience but also could hope to have their voices heard.

NOTES

1. Kim Knott, "Women Researching, Women Researched: Gender as an Issue in the Empirical Study of Religion," in Ursula King, ed., *Religion and Gender* (Oxford: Blackwell, 1995), p. 206.

2. See, e.g., Dolores S. Williams, *Sisters in the Wilderness: The Challenge of Womanist God-Talk* (Maryknoll, N.Y.: Orbis Books, 1993), p. 189.

3. Patricia J. Higgins, "Women in the Islamic Republic of Iran: Legal, Social and Ideological Changes," *Signs: Journal of Women in Culture and Society*, vol. 10 (1985), p. 493. See also Fatima Mernissi, "Femininity as Subversion: Reflection on the Muslim Concept of Nushuz," in Diana L. Eck and Devaki Jain, eds., *Speaking of Faith: Global Perspectives on Women, Religion and Social Change* (Philadelphia, Pa.: New Society Publishers, 1987), p. 96.

4. See Mernissi, "Femininity," p. 106.

5. Debra Renee Kaufmann, "Paradoxical Politics: Gender Politics Among Newly Orthodox Jewish Women in the United States," in Valentine M. Moghadam, ed., *Identity Politics and Women: Cultural Reassertions and Feminisms in International Perspective* (Boulder, Colo: Westview Press, 1994), pp. 351, 360–61.

6. Karma Lekshe Tsomo, ed., *Sakyadhita: Daughters of the Buddha* (Ithaca, N.Y.: Snow Lion Publications, 1988), pp. 208, 322–23.

7. Tsomo, *Sakyadhita*, pp. 23–29. See also Bhadantacariya Buddhaghosa, *The Path of Purification: Visuddhimagga*, 5th ed., tr. Bhikkhu-Nanamoli (Berkeley, Calif.: Shambala Publications, 1991), p. 829 n. 4.

8. For a good summary, see Chilla Bulbeck, "Hearing the Difference: First and Third World Feminisms," *Asian Studies Review*, vol. 15 (1991), pp. 77–91.

9. See, e.g., Madhu Kishwar, "A Horror of Isms," in Mary Evans, ed., *The Woman Question* (London: Sage Publications, 1994), p. 23.

10. See Wazir Jahan Karim, *Women and Culture: Between Malay Adat and Islam* (Boulder, Colo.: Westview Press, 1992), p. 227, on this issue related to the practice of veiling in Malaysia.

11. Moghadam, *Identity Politics,* p. ix.

12. Moghadam, *Identity Politics,* p. ix.

13. Emancipation of Women, "The Veil and the Question of Women in Iran," in Azar Tabari and Nahid Yeganeh, eds., *In the Shadow of Islam: The Women's Movement in Iran* (London: Zed Press, 1982), pp. 166–67.

14. Leila Ahmed, *Women and Gender in Islam: Historical Roots of a Modern Debate* (New Haven, Conn.: Yale University Press, 1992), p. 199.

15. Ahmed, *Women,* p. 201.

16. Geraldine Brooks, *Nine Parts of Desire: The Hidden World of Islamic Women* (New York: Anchor, 1995), p. 8.

17. John S. Hawley, "Hinduism: Sati and Its Defenders," in John S. Hawley, ed., *Fundamentalism and Gender* (New York: Oxford University Press, 1994), p. 93.

18. Brooks, *Nine Parts,* pp. 232–33.

19. See the helpful summary of positions and opinions in Elisabeth Schüssler Fiorenza, "Feminist Hermeneutics," in David Noel Freedman, ed., *Anchor Bible Dictionary,* vol. 2 (New York: Doubleday, 1992), pp. 783–91.

20. Rita M. Gross, *Buddhism After Patriarchy: A Feminist History, Analysis, and Reconstruction of Buddhism* (Albany: State University of New York Press, 1993), p. 282. See the opposite view in Tsomo's *Sakyadhita*: "Another supposition is that, whether a person interested in enlightenment is a woman or a man, it generally is more efficient to work toward their goal unencumbered by the distractions of family life" (p. 19).

21. June Campbell, *Traveller in Space: In Search of Female Identity in Tibetan Buddhism* (London: Athlone, 1996), p. 185.

22. Tsultrim Allione, *Women of Wisdom* (London: Arkana, 1986), pp. 5–6. However, she goes on to somehow contradict this with a more subtle understanding of the nature of suffering and the function of the ego and false discrimination between self and other (p. 26).

23. Chatsumarn Kabilsingh, "Nuns of Thailand," in Tsomo, *Sakyadhita,* p. 146.

24. See especially Purkiss' first chapter, entitled "A Holocaust of One's Own: The Myth of the Burning Times," in Diane Purkiss, *The Witch in History: Early Modern and Twentieth-century Representations* (London: Routledge, 1996), pp. 7–29.

25. Williams, *Sisters,* pp. 189–91.

26. See also Jo Ann Hackett, "Can A Sexist Model Liberate Us? Ancient Near Eastern 'Fertility' Goddesses," *Journal of Feminist Studies in Religion*, vol. 5 (1989), p. 67–68, and Katherine Young, "Goddesses, Feminists and Scholars," in Arvind Sharma and Katherine Young, eds., *The Annual Review of Women in World Religions*, vol. 1 (Albany: State University of New York Press, 1991), pp. 105–79.

27. Tsomo, *Sakyadhita*, p. 325.

28. Tsomo, *Sakyadhita*, p. 19.

29. Interestingly, Susan Starr Sered (*Priestess, Mother, Sacred Sister: Religions Dominated by Women*, New York: Oxford University Press, 1994) finds that of all the women's religions, only that group which she characterizes as Feminist Spirituality worships goddesses (p. 173). By comparison, Christian Science, Shakers, and Spiritualism have androgynous deities (p. 174–76).

30. Parts of this section appeared in another form in Majella Franzmann, "Presidential Address. Against the Tyranny of Tolerance: Some Thoughts on Personal and Intellectual Integrity in Hermeneutical Practice," *Australian Religion Studies Review*, vol. 9/2 (1996), pp. 1–9.

31. See Knott's ("Women," *passim*) reflections along the same lines about her own research and the crucial issue of personal and intellectual honesty.

32. Of course, we could move further back to ask about the prejudices that give rise to the judgments. Gadamer writes of legitimate and illegitimate prejudices and the task of critical reasoning in overcoming all the illegitimate ones (Hans-Georg Gadamer, "The Historicity of Understanding," in K. Mueller-Vollmer, ed., *The Hermeneutics Reader: Texts of the German Tradition from the Enlightenment to the Present*, Oxford: Blackwell, 1986, p. 261). Bultmann distinguishes between a dogmatic prejudice that purports to be a definitive understanding and a preunderstanding that is open and set in the life context of the interpreter (Rudolf Bultmann, "Hermeneutics and Theology," in Mueller-Vollmer, *Hermeneutics Reader*, p. 245).

33. Alan Buchanan, "Judging the Past: The Case of the Human Radiation Experiments," *Hastings Centre Report*, May–June (1996), p. 26.

34. Majella Franzmann, "The City as Woman: The Case of Babylon in Isaiah 47," *Australian Biblical Review*, vol. 43 (1995), pp. 1–19.

35. Detweiler and Robbins' description of Ricoeur's hermeneutical method is particularly apt in this regard, outlining Ricoeur's "firm openness to the examination of many positions from the tentative adoption of one of them, in the expectation of receiving correction and offering

correction as well. This is a stance more open-minded and open-ended than that of the poststructuralists who have already closed off the dialogue . . . by presupposing the singular validity of deconstructive tactics . . .”; R. Detweiler and V. K. Robbins, “From New Criticism to Post-structuralism: Twentieth-Century Hermeneutics,” in S. Prickett, ed., *Reading the Text: Biblical Criticism and Literary Theory* (Oxford: Blackwell, 1991), p. 270.

36. T. Hoy, *Praxis, Truth, and Liberation: Essays on Gadamer, Taylor, Polanyi, Habermas, Gutierrez, and Ricoeur* (Lanham, Md.: University Press of America, 1988), p. 104.

37. See S. D. Lane and R. A. Rubinstein, “Judging the Other: Responding to Traditional Female Genital Surgeries,” *Hastings Centre Report*, May–June (1996), p. 37.

38. Sarah L. Hoagland, *Lesbian Ethics: Toward New Value* (Palo Alto, Calif.: Institute of Lesbian Studies, 1988), pp. 235–41. With this concept of “autokoenonous,” Hoagland seems to come close to the idea of the sense of community.

Suggested Readings

Hermeneutics

Palmer, Richard E. *Hermeneutics: Interpretation Theory in Schleiermacher, Dilthey, Heidegger, and Gadamer.* Evanston, Ill.: Northwestern University Press, 1969.

Part I gives a good overview of modern theories about hermeneutics, especially section 3, "Six Modern Definitions of Hermeneutics" (pp. 33–45). There is also a good section on the debate about objectivity in interpretation between Betti and Gadamer (pp. 58–59), and two sections on what is experience in relation to Dilthey (pp. 108–9) but especially in relation to Gadamer and his dialectical hermeneutics (pp. 194–201).

Grondin, Jean, *Introduction to Philosophical Hermeneutics.* Yale Studies in Hermeneutics, New Haven, Conn.: Yale University Press, 1994.

———. *Sources of Hermeneutics.* SUNY Series in Contemporary Continental Philosophy, Albany, N.Y.: State University of New York Press, 1995.

These two volumes of Grondin are more recent than Palmer's book, although the German version of the first appeared in 1991. The first is probably of more help to the introductory student than the second. It is broader in scope than Palmer but I do not think it is as easy for the student to read.

Mueller-Vollmer, K., ed. *The Hermeneutics Reader: Texts of the German Tradition from the Enlightenment to the Present.* Oxford: Blackwell, 1986.

This is a good volume for getting an idea of the range of thinking about hermeneutics, although it is not always an easy read. As Palmer notes (p. xiii), most of the primary material for studying hermeneutics is in German, so it is helpful for the student to have an introduction like his or the Mueller-Vollmer volume of English translations of German works.

Two entries in *The Anchor Bible Dictionary* may be useful; the first, on the general meaning of the term *hermeneutics* and the second, on *feminist hermeneutics*:

Lategan, Bernard C. "Hermeneutics," in David Noel Freedman, ed., *The Anchor Bible Dictionary*, vol. 3. New York: Doubleday, 1992, pp. 149–54.

Fiorenza, Elisabeth Schüssler. "Feminist Hermeneutics," in David Noel Freedman, ed., *The Anchor Bible Dictionary*, vol. 2. New York: Doubleday, 1992, pp. 783–91.

Anthologies of Women's Religious Writings

There are now a number of useful anthologies, though much of the writing is limited to Christian or Jewish women.

CHRISTIAN/JEWISH/NORTH AMERICAN/WESTERN

Clark, Elizabeth, and Herbert Richardson, eds. *Women and Religion: A Feminist Sourcebook of Christian Thought.* New York: Harper & Row, 1977.

Herschel, Susannah, ed. *On Being a Jewish Feminist: A Reader.* New York: Schocken Books, 1983.

Kaye/Kantrowitz, Melanie, and Irena Klepfisz, eds. *The Tribe of Dina: A Jewish Women's Anthology.* Boston: Beacon Press, 1989.

Loades, Ann, ed. *Feminist Theology: A Reader.* London/Louisville, Ky.: SPCK/Westminster/John Knox Press, 1990.

Plaskow, Judith, and Carol Christ, eds. *Weaving the Visions: New Patterns in Feminist Spirituality.* New York: HarperSanFrancisco, 1989.

Young, Serenity. *An Anthology of Sacred Texts by and About Women.* New York: Crossroad, 1993.

CLASSICAL

Kraemer, Ross Shepard, ed. *Maenads, Martyrs, Matrons, Monastics: A Sourcebook of Women's Religions in the Greco-Roman World.* Philadelphia: Fortress Press, 1988.

MEDIEVAL

Wilson, Katharina M., ed. *Medieval Women Writers.* Athens: University of Georgia Press, 1984.

Examples of Women's Personal Writing from Within Particular Traditions or Across Traditions

Daly, Mary. *Outercourse: The be-dazzling voyage containing recollections from my logbook of a radical feminist philosopher (be-ing an account of my time/space travels and ideas—then again, and now and how).* Melbourne: Spinifex, 1993.

Hurcombe, Linda, ed. *Sex and God: Some Varieties of Women's Religious Experience.* New York: Routledge & Kegan Paul, 1987.

O'Halloran, Maura 'Soshin.' *Pure Heart Enlightened Mind: The Zen Journal and Letters of an Irish Woman in Japan.* London: Thorsons, 1994.

The Quaker Women's Group. *Bringing the Invisible into the Light: Some Quaker Feminists Speak of Their Experience.* Swarthmore Lecture Series, London: Quaker Home Service, 1986.

Tsomo, Karma Lekshe, ed. *Sakyadhita: Daughters of the Buddha.* Ithaca, N.Y.: Snow Lion Publications, 1988.

Material on Women's Religious Experience from a Broad Spectrum of Cross-cultural and Religious Systems

Hoch-Smith, Judith, and Anita Spring, eds. *Women in Ritual and Symbolic Roles.* New York/London: Plenum Press, 1978.

King, Ursula. *Women in the World's Religions, Past and Present.* New York: Paragon House, 1987.

Sharma, Arvind, ed. *Today's Woman in World Religions.* Albany: State University of New York Press, 1994.

Sharma, Arvind, and Katherine Young, eds. *The Annual Review of Women in World Religions,* vol. 1. Albany: State University of New York Press, 1991.

————. *The Annual Review of Women in World Religions,* vol. 2. Albany: State University of New York Press, 1992.

Some of the hardest material for the student to get hold of is from Third World women, though that situation is changing rapidly. For specifically feminist theology from Third World women:

Fabella, Virginia, ed. *With Passion and Compassion: Third World Women Doing Theology. Reflections from the Women's Commission of the Ecumenical Association of Third World Theologians.* Maryknoll, N.Y.: Orbis Books, 1988.

Falk, Nancy, and Rita Gross. *Unspoken Worlds: Women's Religious Lives in Non-Western Cultures.* San Francisco: Harper & Row, 1980.

King, Ursula, ed. *Feminist Theology from the Third World: A Reader.* London/Maryknoll, N.Y.: SPCK/Orbis Books, 1994. King comments that this book offers a much wider and more diverse range of sources than Virginia Fabella's *With Passion and Compassion.* The introduction offers a good overview of the newer history of development of Third World feminist theology (pp. 1–20).

Russell, Letty M., Kwok Pui-Lan, Ada María Isasi-Díaz, and Katie Geneva Cannon. *Inheriting Our Mothers' Gardens: Feminist Theology in Third World Perspective.* Philadelphia: Westminster Press, 1988. This is mostly from women of color doing feminist theology in the context of the United States.

Bibliographies

Kadel, Andrew. *Matrology: A Bibliography of Writings by Christian Women from the First to the Fifteenth Centuries.* New York: Continuum, 1995.

King, Ursula. *Women and Spirituality: Voices of Protest and Promise.* Women and Society, London: Macmillan Education, 1989. This book has an extensive bibliography.

Of course there are the more general bibliographical references to be found in the Indexes Database of the American Theological Library Association. These are generally easy to come by.

Especially useful is Thomas P. Fenton and Mary J. Heffron, *Women in the Third World: A Directory of Resources* (Maryknoll, N.Y.: Orbis Books, 1987). This publication gives references to women's own stories but also provides addresses for organizations from which up-to-date information might be obtained. Although it focuses on the Third World, some entries can be used for more general information. Thus the *Women's Review of Books* is often very useful for general review articles on women's spiritual/religious writing.

Bibliography

—m—

Ahmed, Akbar S. *Pakistan Society: Islam, Ethnicity and Leadership in South Asia.* Oxford: Oxford University Press, 1986.

Ahmed, Leila. "Women and the Advent of Islam," *Signs: Journal of Women in Culture and Society,* vol. 11 (1986), pp. 665–91.

———. *Women and Gender in Islam: Historical Roots of a Modern Debate.* New Haven, Conn.: Yale University Press, 1992.

Allione, Tsultrim. *Women of Wisdom.* London: Arkana, 1986.

Apel, Karl-Otto. "Perspectives for a General Hermeneutic Theory," in K. Mueller-Vollmer, ed., *The Hermeneutics Reader: Texts of the German Tradition from the Enlightenment to the Present.* Oxford: Blackwell, 1986, pp. 321–45.

Armour, Ellen T. "Questioning 'Woman' in Feminist/Womanist Theology: Irigaray, Ruether, and Daly," in C. W. Maggie Kim et al., eds., *Transfigurations: Theology and the French Feminists.* Minneapolis: Fortress Press, 1993, pp. 143–69.

Augustine. "The Confessions," in Whitney J. Oates, ed., *Basic Writings of Saint Augustine,* vol. 1. New York: Random House, 1948, pp. 1–256.

Babb, Lawrence A. "Indigenous Feminism in a Modern Hindu Sect," in Rehana Ghadially, ed., *Women in Indian Society: A Reader.* New Delhi: Sage Publications, 1988, pp. 270–87.

Bancroft, Anne. *Weavers of Wisdom: Women of the Twentieth Century.* London: Arkana, 1989.

———. *Women in Search of the Sacred.* London: Arkana, 1996.

Barnes, Nancy Schuster. "Buddhism," in Arvind Sharma, ed., *Women in World Religions.* McGill Studies in the History of Religions, Albany: State University of New York Press, 1987, pp. 105–33.

———. "Women in Buddhism," in Arvind Sharma, ed., *Today's Woman in World Religions.* Albany: State University of New York Press, 1994, pp. 137–69.

See also Schuster, Nancy.

Beck, Lois, and Nikki Keddie, eds. *Women in the Muslim World.* Cambridge, Mass.: Harvard University Press, 1978.

Bernal, Victoria. "Gender, Culture, and Capitalism: Women and the Remaking of Islamic 'Tradition' in a Sudanese Village," *Comparative Studies in Society and History,* vol. 36 (1994), pp. 36–67.

Briggs, Sheila. "Sexual Justice and the 'Righteousness of God,' " in Linda Hurcombe, ed., *Sex and God: Some Varieties of Women's Religious Experience.* New York: Routledge & Kegan Paul, 1987, pp. 251–77.

Brooks, Geraldine. *Nine Parts of Desire: The Hidden World of Islamic Women.* New York: Anchor, 1995.

Bryant, Gwendolyn. "The French Heretic Beguine: Marguerite Porete," in Katharina M. Wilson, ed., *Medieval Women Writers.* Athens: University of Georgia Press, 1984, pp. 204–26.

Buchanan, A. "Judging the Past: The Case of the Human Radiation Experiments," *Hastings Centre Report* (May–June 1996), pp. 25–30.

Buddhaghosa, Bhadantacariya. *The Path of Purification: Visuddhimagga,* 5th ed., translated by Bhikkhu Nanamoli. Berkeley, Calif.: Shambala Publications, 1991.

Bulbeck, Chilla. "Hearing the Difference: First and Third World Feminisms," *Asian Studies Review,* vol. 15 (1991), pp. 77–91.

Bultmann, Rudolf. "Hermeneutics and Theology," in K. Mueller-Vollmer, ed., *The Hermeneutics Reader: Texts of the German Tradition from the Enlightenment to the Present.* Oxford: Blackwell, 1986, pp. 242–55.

Bynum, Caroline Walker. "The Female Body and Religious Practice in the Later Middle Ages," in Michel Feher, Ramona Naddaff, Nachia Tazi, eds., *Fragments for a History of the Human Body. Part 1.* New York: Zone, 1989, pp. 160–219.

Byrne, Lavinia, ed. *The Hidden Tradition: Women's Spiritual Writings Rediscovered.* London: SPCK, 1991.

Callaway, Barbara, and Lucy Creevey. *The Heritage of Islam: Women, Religion, and Politics in West Africa.* Boulder, Colo.: Lynne Rienner, 1994.

Campbell, June. *Traveller in Space: In Search of Female Identity in Tibetan Buddhism.* London: Athlone, 1996.

Cantor, Aviva. *Jewish Women, Jewish Men: The Legacy of Patriarchy in Jewish Life.* New York: HarperSanFrancisco, 1995.

Carmody, Denise Lardner. *Women and World Religions,* 2nd ed. Englewood Cliffs, N.J.: Prentice-Hall, 1989.

———. *Religious Woman: Contemporary Reflections on Eastern Texts.* New York: Crossroad, 1991.

———. *Mythological Woman: Contemporary Reflections on Ancient Religious Stories.* New York: Crossroad, 1992.

Castelli, Elizabeth A. "Elisabeth Schüssler Fiorenza on Women in the Gospels and Feminist Christology," *Religious Studies Review,* vol. 22 (1996), pp. 296–300.

Christ, Carol P. *Diving Deep and Surfacing: Women Writers on Spiritual Quest,* 2nd ed. Boston: Beacon Press, 1986.

Christ, Carol, and Judith Plaskow, eds. *Womanspirit Rising: A Feminist Reader in Religion.* San Francisco: Harper & Row, 1979.

Coe, George Albert. *The Psychology of Religion.* Chicago: University of Chicago Press, 1916.

Condren, Mary. *The Serpent and the Goddess: Women, Religion, and Power in Celtic Ireland.* San Francisco: Harper & Row, 1989.

Conn, Joann Wolski, ed. *Women's Spirituality: Resources for Christian Development.* New York: Paulist, 1986.

Daly, Mary. *Gyn/Ecology: The Metaethics of Radical Feminism.* Boston: Beacon Press, 1978.

———. *Pure Lust: Elemental Feminist Philosophy.* London: Women's Press, 1984.

———. *Outercourse: The be-dazzling voyage containing recollections from my logbook of a radical feminist philosopher (be-ing an account of my time/space travels and ideas—then again, and now and how).* Melbourne: Spinifex, 1993.

Davis, Elizabeth, and Carol Leonard. *The Women's Wheel of Life: Thirteen Archetypes of Woman at Her Fullest Power.* Rydalmere, NSW: Hodder and Stoughton, 1996.

Detweiler, R., and Robbins, V. K. "From New Criticism to Poststructuralism: Twentieth-Century Hermeneutics," in S. Prickett, ed., *Reading the Text: Biblical Criticism and Literary Theory.* Oxford: Blackwell, 1991, pp. 225–80.

Dhruvarajan, Vanaja. *Hindu Women and the Power of Ideology*. Granby, Mass.: Bergin & Garvey, 1989.

Doi, 'Abdur Rahman I. *Women in Shari'ah (Islamic Law)*, 2nd ed., revised and edited by Abdalhaqq Bewley. London: Ta-Ha, 1992.

Douglas, Mary. *Purity and Danger: An Analysis of Concepts of Pollution and Taboo*. Harmondsworth, U.K.: Penguin, 1970.

Dwyer, Daisy Hilse. "Women, Sufism, and Decision-making in Moroccan Islam," in Lois Beck and Nikki Keddie, eds., *Women in the Muslim World*. Cambridge, Mass.: Harvard University Press, 1978, pp. 585–98.

Eck, Diana L., and Devaki Jain, eds. *Speaking of Faith: Global Perspectives on Women, Religion and Social Change*. Philadelphia: New Society Publishers, 1987.

Emancipation of Women. "The Veil and the Question of Women in Iran," in Azar Tabari and Nahid Yeganeh, eds., *In the Shadow of Islam: The Women's Movement in Iran*. London: Zed Press, 1982, pp. 156–68.

Engineer, Asghar Ali, ed. *The Status of Women in Islam*. Delhi: Ajanta Publications, 1987.

————. *The Rights of Women in Islam*. New Delhi: Sterling Publishers, 1992.

Ernst, Carl. "Lives of Sufi Saints," in Donald S. Lopez Jr., ed., *Religions of India in Practice*. Princeton, N.J.: Princeton University Press, 1995, pp. 495–512.

Evans, Mary, ed. *The Woman Question*, 2nd ed. London: Sage Publications, 1994.

Falk, Nancy, and Rita Gross. *Unspoken Worlds: Women's Religious Lives in Non-Western Cultures*, 2nd ed. Belmont, Calif.: Wadsworth, 1989.

Farnham, Suzanne G., et al. *Listening Hearts: Discerning Call in Community*. Harrisburg, Pa.: Morehouse, 1991.

Ferguson, Ann. "A Feminist Aspect Theory of the Self," in Ann Garry and Marilyn Pearsall, eds., *Women, Knowledge, and Reality: Explorations in Feminist Philosophy*. Boston: Unwin Hyman, 1989, pp. 93–107.

Fernea, Elizabeth Warnock, and Basima Qattan Bezirgan, eds. *Middle Eastern Women Speak*. The Dan Danciger Publication Series, Austin: University of Texas Press, 1977.

Fernea, Robert A., and Elizabeth W. Fernea. "Variation in Religious Observance Among Islamic Women," in Nikki R. Keddie, ed., *Scholars, Saints, and Sufis: Muslim Religious Institutions in the Middle East Since 1500*. Berkeley: University of California Press, 1972, pp. 385–401.

Field, Barbara. "The Battle's Won but Not the War—Resistance to Women in Leadership Positions in the Church," *Women–Church*, vol. 14 (1994), pp. 17–19.

Fiorenza, Elisabeth Schüssler. "The Influence of Feminist Theory on My Theological Work," *Journal of Feminist Studies in Religion*, vol. 7 (1991), pp. 95–105.

———. *But She Said: Feminist Practices of Biblical Interpretation*. Boston: Beacon Press, 1992.

———. "Feminist Hermeneutics," in David Noel Freedman, ed., *Anchor Bible Dictionary*, vol. 2. New York: Doubleday, 1992, pp. 783–91.

Flax, Jane. *Thinking Fragments: Psychoanalysis, Feminism, and Postmodernism in the Contemporary West*. Berkeley: University of California Press, 1990.

Franzmann, Majella. "'Cast yourselves recklessly into the current of life!' A Critical Response to Richard Leonard's *Beloved Daughters: 100 Years of Papal Teaching on Women*," *Australian Religion Studies Review*, vol. 8/2 (1995), pp. 104–8.

———. "The City as Woman: The Case of Babylon in Isaiah 47," *Australian Biblical Review*, vol. 43 (1995), pp. 1–19.

———. "AASR 1996 Presidential Address. Against the Tyranny of Tolerance: Some Thoughts on Personal and Intellectual Integrity in Hermeneutical Practice," *Australian Religion Studies Review*, vol. 9/2 (1996), pp. 1–9.

Fuller, Christopher John. *The Camphor Flame: Popular Hinduism in Society in India*. Princeton: Princeton University Press, 1992.

Gadamer, Hans-Georg. *Truth and Method*. New York: Seabury, 1975.

———. "The Historicity of Understanding," in K. Mueller-Vollmer, ed., *The Hermeneutics Reader: Texts of the German Tradition from the Enlightenment to the Present*. Oxford: Blackwell, 1986, pp. 257–92.

Gold, Ann Grodzins. "Devotional Power or Dangerous Magic? The Jungli Rani's Case," in Gloria Goodwin Raheja and Ann Grodzins Gold, *Listen to the Heron's Words: Reimagining Gender and Kinship in North India*. Delhi: Oxford University Press, 1996, pp. 149–63.

Goldman, Robert P. "Foreword," in Padmanabh S. Jaini, *Gender and Salvation: Jaina Debates on the Spiritual Liberation of Women*. Berkeley: University of California Press, 1991, pp. vii–xxiv.

Good, Mary-Jo Del Vecchio. "A Comparative Perspective on Women in Provincial Iran and Turkey," in Lois Beck and Nikki Keddie, eds., *Women in the Muslim World*. Cambridge, Mass.: Harvard University Press, 1978, pp. 629–50.

Graham, Elaine L. *Making the Difference: Gender, Personhood and Theology*. Minneapolis: Fortress Press, 1996.

Graham-Brown, Sarah. *Images of Women: The Portrayal of Women in Pho-*

tography of the Middle East 1860–1950. New York: Columbia University Press, 1988.

Grant, Jacquelyn. *White Women's Christ and Black Women's Jesus: Feminist Christology and Womanist Response.* AAR Academy Series 64, Atlanta, Ga.: Scholars Press, 1989.

Grant, Judith. "I Feel Therefore I Am: A Critique of Female Experience as the Basis for a Feminist Epistemology," *Women and Politics,* vol. 7 (1987), pp. 99–114.

Gross, Rita M. *Buddhism After Patriarchy: A Feminist History, Analysis, and Reconstruction of Buddhism.* Albany: State University of New York Press, 1993.

———. *Feminism and Religion: An Introduction.* Boston: Beacon Press, 1996.

Hackett, Jo Ann. "Can a Sexist Model Liberate Us? Ancient Near Eastern 'Fertility' Goddesses," *Journal of Feminist Studies in Religion,* vol. 5 (1989), pp. 65–76.

Haddad, Yvonne Yazbeck. "Islam, Women and Revolution in Twentieth-Century Arab Thought," in Yvonne Yazbeck Haddad and Ellison Banks Findly, eds., *Women, Religion, and Social Change.* Albany: State University of New York Press, 1985, pp. 275–306.

Hansen, Kathryn. "Heroic Modes of Women in Indian Myth, Ritual and History: The *Tapasvini* and the *Virangana,*" in Arvind Sharma and Katherine Young, eds., *The Annual Review of Women in World Religions,* vol. 2. Albany: State University of New York Press, 1992, pp. 1–62.

Harland, Lindsey. "Abandoning Shame: Mira and the Margins of Marriage," in Lindsey Harland and Paul B. Courtright, eds., *From the Margins of Hindu Marriage: Essays on Gender, Religion, and Culture.* New York: Oxford University Press, 1995, pp. 204–27.

Harvey, Peter. "Buddhism," in Jean Holm and John Bowker, eds., *Human Nature and Destiny.* Themes in Religious Studies, London: Pinter Publishers, 1994, pp. 9–38.

Harvey, Youngsook Kim. *Six Korean Women: The Socialization of Shamans.* St. Paul, Minn.: West Publishing, 1979.

Hawkesworth, Mary E. "Feminist Epistemology: A Survey of the Field", *Women and Politics,* vol. 7 (1987), pp. 115–27.

Hawley, John Stratton. "Hinduism: Sati and Its Defenders," in John S. Hawley, ed., *Fundamentalism and Gender.* New York: Oxford University Press, 1994, pp. 79–110.

Hayes, Diana L. "Different Voices: Black, Womanist and Catholic," in Mary Phil Korsak, ed., *Voicing Identity: Women and Religious Traditions in Europe. Conference Records. Fifth Biennial Conference at the University of*

Louvain, 16–20 August, 1993. Louvain: European Society of Women in Theological Research, pp. 1–34.

Hein, Hilde. "Liberating Philosophy: An End to the Dichotomy of Spirit and Matter," in Ann Garry and Marilyn Pearsall, eds., *Women, Knowledge, and Reality: Explorations in Feminist Philosophy.* Boston: Unwin Hyman, 1989, pp. 293–311.

Hekman, Susan J. *Gender and Knowledge: Elements of a Postmodern Feminism.* Northeastern Series in Femininst Theory, Boston: Northeastern University Press, 1990.

Hennecke, Edgar, Wilhelm Schneemelcher, and R. McL. Wilson, eds. *New Testament Apocrypha. Vol. 1: Gospels and Related Writings.* Philadelphia: Westminster, 1963.

Hermansen, Marcia K. "The Female Hero in the Islamic Religious Tradition," in Arvind Sharma and Katherine Young, eds., *The Annual Review of Women in World Religions*, vol. 2. Albany: State University of New York Press, 1992, pp. 111–43.

Hertel, Bradley R., and Cynthia Ann Humes, eds. *Living Banaras: Hindu Religion in Cultural Context.* Albany: State University of New York Press, 1993.

Hewitt, Marsha Aileen. *Critical Theory of Religion: A Feminist Analysis.* Minneapolis: Fortress Press, 1995.

Higgins, Patricia J. "Women in the Islamic Republic of Iran: Legal, Social and Ideological Changes," *Signs: Journal of Women in Culture and Society*, vol. 10 (1985), pp. 477–94.

Hoagland, Sarah L. *Lesbian Ethics: Toward New Value* (Palo Alto, Calif.: Institute of Lesbian Studies, 1988, pp. 235–41.

Holden, Pat, ed. *Women's Religious Experience.* London: Croom Helm, 1983.

Holm, Jean, and John Bowker, eds. *Women in Religion.* Themes in Religious Studies, London: Pinter, 1994.

hooks, bell. *Feminist Theory: From Margin to Center.* Boston: South End Press, 1984.

Hoy, T. *Praxis, Truth, and Liberation: Essays on Gadamer, Taylor, Polanyi, Habermas, Gutierrez, and Ricoeur.* Lanham, Md.: University Press of America, 1988.

Hughes, Kate Pritchard, ed. *Contemporary Australian Feminism.* Melbourne: Longman Cheshire, 1994.

Humes, Cynthia Ann. "The Goddess of the Vidhyas in Banaras," in Bradley R. Hertel and Cynthia Ann Humes, eds., *Living Banaras: Hindu Religion in Cultural Context.* Albany: State University of New York Press, 1983, pp. 181–204.

Hunt, Mary E. "Friends in Deed," in Linda Hurcombe, ed., *Sex and God: Some Varieties of Women's Religious Experience*. New York: Routledge & Kegan Paul, 1987, pp. 46–54.

Hurcombe, Linda, ed. *Sex and God: Some Varieties of Women's Religious Experience*. New York: Routledge & Kegan Paul, 1987.

Irigaray, Luce. *Speculum of the Other Woman*, tr. Gillian C. Gill. Ithaca, N.Y.: Cornell University Press, 1985.

Jeffery, Patricia. *Frogs in a Well: Indian Women in Purdah*. London: Zed Press, 1979.

Jones, Serene. "'Women's Experience' Between a Rock and a Hard Place: Feminist, Womanist and *Mujerista* Theologies in North America," *Religious Studies Review*, vol. 21 (1995), pp. 171–78.

Joseph, Alison, ed. *Through the Devil's Gateway: Women, Religion and Taboo*. London: SPCK in association with Channel Four, 1990.

Kabilsingh, Chatsumarn. "Nuns of Thailand," in Karma Lekshe Tsomo, *Sakyadhita: Daughters of the Buddha*. Ithaca, N.Y.: Snow Lion Publications, 1988, pp. 145–9.

Kadel, Andrew. *Matrology: A Bibliography of Writings by Christian Women from the First to the Fifteenth Centuries*. New York: Continuum, 1995.

Kapadia, Karin. *Siva and Her Sisters: Gender, Caste, and Class in Rural South India*. Boulder, Colo.: Westview Press, 1995.

Kapleau, Roshi Philip. *Awakening to Zen: The Teachings of Roshi Philip Kapleau*. Sydney: Bantam Books, 1997.

———, ed. *The Three Pillars of Zen: Teaching, Practice, and Enlightenment*. Boston: Beacon Press, 1967.

Karim, Wazir Jahan. *Women and Culture: Between Malay Adat and Islam*. Boulder, Colo.: Westview Press, 1992.

Kaufmann, Debra Renee. "Paradoxical Politics: Gender Politics Among Newly Orthodox Jewish Women in the United States," in Valentine M. Moghadam, ed., *Identity Politics and Women: Cultural Reassertions and Feminisms in International Perspective*. Boulder, Colo.: Westview Press, 1994, pp. 349–66.

Kaye/Kantrowitz, Melanie, and Irena Klepfisz, eds. *The Tribe of Dina: A Jewish Women's Anthology*. Boston: Beacon Press, 1989.

Kendall, Laurel. *Shamans, Housewives, and Other Restless Spirits: Women in Korean Ritual Life*. Honolulu: University of Hawaii Press, 1985.

Kersenboom-Story, Saskia C. *Nityasumangali Devadasi Tradition in South India*. Delhi: Motilal Banarsidass, 1987.

Kim, C. W. Maggie, et al. *Transfigurations: Theology and the French Feminists*. Minneapolis: Fortress Press, 1993.

King, Ursula, ed. *Women in the World's Religions, Past and Present.* New York: Paragon House, 1987.

———. *Women and Spirituality: Voices of Protest and Promise.* Women and Society, London: Macmillan Education, 1989.

Kinsley, David. "Devotion as an Alternative to Marriage in the Lives of Some Hindu Women Devotees," *Journal of Asian and African Studies,* vol. 15 (1980), pp. 83–93.

Kishwar, Madhu. "A Horror of Isms," in Mary Evans, ed., *The Woman Question.* London: Sage Publications, 1994, pp. 22–29.

Knott, Kim. "Women Researching, Women Researched: Gender as an Issue in the Empirical Study of Religion," in Ursula King, ed., *Religion and Gender.* Oxford: Blackwell, 1995, pp. 199–218.

Kondoleon, Christine. *Domestic and Divine: Roman Mosaics in the House of Dionysos.* Ithaca/London: Cornell University Press, 1995.

Kraemer, Ross Shepard, ed. *Maenads, Martyrs, Matrons, Monastics: A Sourcebook of Women's Religions in the Greco-Roman World.* Philadelphia: Fortress Press, 1988.

Lane, S. D., and R. A. Rubinstein. "Judging the Other: Responding to Traditional Female Genital Surgeries," *Hastings Centre Report,* (May–June 1996), pp. 31–39.

Lategan, Bernard C. "Hermeneutics," in David Noel Freedman, ed., *The Anchor Bible Dictionary,* vol. 3. New York: Doubleday, 1992, pp. 149–54.

Leslie, I. Julia. "Essence and Existence: Women and Religion in Ancient Indian Texts," in Pat Holden, ed., *Women's Religious Experience.* London: Croom Helm, 1983, pp. 89–112.

———. *The Perfect Wife: The Orthodox Hindu Woman According to the "Stridharmapaddhati" of Tryambakayajvan.* Oxford University South Asian Studies Series, New York: Oxford University Press, 1989.

———. *Roles and Rituals for Hindu Women.* London: Pinter, 1991.

Lopez Jr., Donald S., ed. *Religions of India in Practice.* Princeton, N.J.: Princeton University Press, 1995.

Lorde, Audre. "An Open Letter to Mary Daly," in Cherríe Moraga and Gloria Anzaldúa, eds., *This Bridge Called My Back: Writings by Radical Women of Color,* 2nd ed. New York: Kitchen Table: Women of Color Press, 1983, pp. 94–97.

Magee, Penny. "Sex and Secularism: Indian Women and the Politics of Religious Discourse," in Morny Joy and Penny Magee, eds., *Claiming Our Rites: Studies in Religion by Australian Women Scholars.* Adelaide: AASR, 1994, pp. 157–85.

Maitland, Sara. "Passionate Prayer: Masochistic Images in Women's Experience," in Linda Hurcombe, ed., *Sex and God: Some Varieties of Women's Religious Experience*. New York: Routledge & Kegan Paul, 1987, pp. 125–40.

Mananzan, Mary John, ed. *Woman and Religion*. Manila: Institute of Women's Studies, St. Scholastica's College, 1992.

Manasra, Najah. "Palestinian Women: Between Tradition and Revolution," in Ebba Augustin, ed., *Palestinian Women: Identity and Experience*. London: Zed Books, 1993, pp. 7–21.

Marcus, Julie. *A World of Difference: Islam and Gender Hierarchy in Turkey*. St. Leonards, NSW: Allen & Unwin, 1992.

Marett, R. R. "Tabu," in James Hastings, ed., *Encyclopaedia of Religion and Ethics*, vol. 12. Edinburgh: T. & T. Clark, 1926, pp. 181–85.

Marglin, Frédérique Apffel. *Wives of the God-King: The Rituals of the Devadasis of Puri*. New York: Oxford University Press, 1985.

———. "Female Sexuality in the Hindu World," in Clarissa W. Atkinson et al., eds., *Immaculate and Powerful: The Female in Sacred Image and Social Reality*. Wellingborough, U.K.: Crucible, 1987, pp. 39–60.

Mayer, Elizabeth Lloyd. "Appendix: An Appraisal of the Psychology of Women in Personality Theories: Freud, Reich, Adler, and Jung," in James Fadiman and Robert Frager, eds., *Personality and Personal Growth*. New York: Harper & Row, 1976, pp. 461–72.

McCance, Dawn. "Projecting a Future for Religious Feminist Criticism," in Klaus K. Klostermaier and Larry W. Furtado, eds., *Religious Studies: Issues, Prospects, and Proposals*. Atlanta, Ga: Scholars Press, 1991, pp. 381–407.

McDaniel, June. "A Holy Woman of Calcutta," in Donald S. Lopez Jr., ed., *Religions of India in Practice*. Princeton, N.J.: Princeton University Press, 1995, pp. 418–25.

Mellor, Philip A. "Self and Suffering: Deconstruction and Reflexive Definition in Buddhism and Christianity," *Religious Studies*, vol. 27 (1991), pp. 49–63.

Mellor, Philip A., and Chris Shilling. *Re-forming the Body: Religion, Community and Modernity*. London: Sage Publications, 1997.

Mernissi, Fatima. *Beyond the Veil: Male-Female Dynamics in Muslim Society*. London: Al Saqi, 1985.

———. "Femininity as Subversion: Reflection on the Muslim Concept of Nushuz," in Diana L. Eck and Devaki Jain, eds., *Speaking of Faith: Global Perspectives on Women, Religion and Social Change*. Philadelphia: New Society Publishers, 1987, pp. 95–108.

————. *Doing Daily Battle: Interviews with Moroccan Women.* London: The Women's Press, 1988.

————. *The Veil and the Male Elite: A Feminist Interpretation of Women's Rights in Islam.* Reading, Mass.: Addison-Wesley, 1991.

Miller-McLemore, Bonnie J. "Epistemology or Bust: A Maternal Feminist Knowledge of Knowing," *The Journal of Religion,* vol. 72 (1992), pp. 229–47.

————. *Also a Mother: Work and Family as Theological Dilemma.* Nashville, Tenn.: Abingdon, 1994.

Millett, Kate. *Sexual Politics.* London: Rupert Hart-Davis, 1971.

Millot, Catherine. "The Feminine Superego," in Parveen Adams and Elizabeth Cowie, eds., *The Woman in Question: m/f.* London: Verso, 1990, pp. 294–314.

Minces, Juliette. *The House of Obedience: Women in Arab Society.* London: Zed Books, 1982.

Moghadam, Valentine M., ed. *Identity Politics and Women: Cultural Reassertions and Feminisms in International Perspective.* Boulder, Colo.: Westview Press, 1994.

Morsy, Soheir A. "Sex Differences and Folk Illness in an Egyptian Village," in Lois Beck and Nikki Keddie, eds., *Women in the Muslim World.* Cambridge, Mass.: Harvard University Press, 1978, pp. 599–616.

Mosala, Itumeleng. "The Implications of the Text of Esther for African Women's Struggle for Liberation in South Africa," *Semeia,* vol. 59 (1992), pp. 129–37.

Mukherjee, Prabhati. *Hindu Women: Normative Models.* New Delhi: Orient Longman, 1978.

Narasimhan, Sakuntala. *Sati: A Study of Widow Burning in India.* New Delhi: Viking, 1990.

O'Halloran, Maura 'Soshin.' *Pure Heart Enlightened Mind: The Zen Journal and Letters of an Irish Woman in Japan.* London: Thorsons, 1994.

O'Neill, Maura. *Women Speaking, Women Listening: Women in Interreligious Dialogue.* Maryknoll, N.Y.: Orbis Books, 1990.

Owen, Alex. *The Darkened Room: Women, Power, and Spiritualism in Late Nineteenth Century England.* London: Virago, 1989.

Ozment, Steven E. *Protestants.* London: Fontana, 1993.

Ozorak, Elizabeth Weiss. "The Power, but Not the Glory: How Women Empower Themselves Through Religion," *Journal for the Scientific Study of Religion,* vol. 35 (1996), pp. 17–29.

The Personal Narratives Group, eds. *Interpreting Women's Lives: Feminist*

Theory and Personal Narratives. Bloomington: Indiana University Press, 1989.

Phillimore, Peter. "Unmarried Women of the Dhaula Dhar: Celibacy and Social Control in Northwest India," *Journal of Anthropological Research*, vol. 47 (1991), pp. 331–50.

Plant, Judith, ed. *Healing the Wounds: The Promise of Ecofeminism*. Philadelphia: New Society Publishers, 1989.

Purkiss, Diane. *The Witch in History: Early Modern and Twentieth-century Representations*. London: Routledge, 1996.

Puttick, Elizabeth. *Women in New Religions: In Search of Community, Sexuality and Spiritual Power*. Houndmills, Basingstoke, U.K.: Macmillan, 1997.

Quaker Women's Group. *Bringing the Invisible into the Light: Some Quaker Feminists Speak of Their Experience*. Swarthmore Lecture Series, London: Quaker Home Service, 1986.

Rahman, Afzalur. *The Role of Muslim Woman in Society*. London: Seerah Foundation, 1986.

Ram, Kalpana. *Mukkuvar Women: Gender, Hegemony and Capitalist Transformation in a Southern Indian Fishing Community*. Sydney: Allen and Unwin, 1991.

Richard, Yann. *Shi'ite Islam*, tr. Antonia Nevill. Cambridge: Blackwell, 1995.

Ricoeur, Paul. *From Text to Action: Essays in Hermeneutics, II*. London: Athlone, 1991.

Robinson, Sandra P. "Hindu Paradigms of Women: Images and Values," in Yvonne Yazbeck Haddad and Ellison Banks Findly, eds., *Women, Religion, and Social Change*. Albany: State University of New York Press, 1985, pp. 181–216.

Ross, Anne. "The Divine Hag of the Pagan Celts," in Venetia Newall, ed., *The Witch Figure: Folklore Essays by a Group of Scholars in England Honouring the 75th Birthday of Katharine M. Briggs*. London: Routledge & Kegan Paul, 1973, pp. 139–64.

Roy, Manisha. *Bengali Women*. Chicago: University of Chicago Press, 1975.

Roy, Shibani. *The Status of Muslim Women in North India*. Delhi: B. R. Publishing, 1979.

Ruether, Rosemary Radford. *Gaia and God: An Ecofeminist Theology of Earth Healing*. New York: HarperSan Francisco, 1992.

Russell, Letty M. *Human Liberation in a Feminist Perspective—A Theology*. Philadelphia: Westminster, 1974.

————. *Church in the Round: Feminist Interpretation of the Church*. Louisville, Ky.: Westminster/John Knox Press, 1993.

Salgado, Nirmala S. "Equality and Inequality in Hinduism and Buddhism," in R. Siriwardena, ed., *Equality and the Religious Traditions of Asia*. London: Pinter, 1987, pp. 51–73.

Samuel, Geoffrey. "The Body in Buddhist and Hindu Tantra: Some Notes," *Religion*, vol. 19 (1989), pp. 197–210.

Schechner, Richard. "Crossing the Water: Pilgrimage, Movement, and Environmental Scenography of the *Ramlila* of Ramnagar," in Bradley R. Hertel and Cynthia Ann Humes, *Living Banaras: Hindu Religion in Cultural Context*. Albany: State University of New York Press, 1993, pp. 19–72.

Schuster, Nancy. "Striking a Balance: Women and Images of Women in Early Chinese Buddhism," in Yvonne Yazbeck Haddad and Ellison Banks Findly, eds., *Women, Religion, and Social Change*. Albany: State University of New York Press, 1985, pp. 87–114.

Selway, Deborah. *Women of Spirit: Contemporary Religious Leaders in Australia*. Melbourne: Longman, 1995.

Sered, Susan Starr. *Priestess, Mother, Sacred Sister: Religions Dominated by Women*. New York: Oxford University Press, 1994.

Shaaban, Bouthaina. *Both Right and Left Handed: Arab Women Talk About Their Lives*. London: The Women's Press, 1988.

Sharma, Arvind, ed. *Today's Woman in World Religions*. Albany: State University of New York Press, 1994.

Sharma, Arvind, and Katherine Young, eds. *The Annual Review of Women in World Religions*, vol. 1. Albany: State University of New York Press, 1991.

————. *The Annual Review of Women in World Religions*, vol. 2. Albany: State University of New York Press, 1992.

Shaw, Miranda. *Passionate Enlightenment: Women in Tantric Buddhism*. Princeton, N.J.: Princeton University Press, 1994.

Smith, Jean. *Tapu Removal in Maori Religion*. Wellington: The Polynesian Society, 1974.

Smith, Margaret. "Rabi'a the Mystic," in Elizabeth Warnock Fernea and Basima Qattan Bezirgan, eds., *Middle Eastern Women Speak*. Austin: University of Texas Press, 1977 [reprint of 1928 ed.], pp. 37–66.

Soper, Kate. "Feminism, Humanism and Postmodernism," in Mary Evans, ed., *The Woman Question*, 2nd ed. London: Sage Publications, 1994, pp. 10–21.

Sponberg, Alan. "Attitudes Toward Women and the Feminine in Early Buddhism," in José Ignacio Cabezón, ed., *Buddhism, Sexuality, and Gender.* Albany: State University of New York Press, 1992, pp. 3–36.

Starhawk. "Feminist, Earth-based Spirituality and Ecofeminism," in Judith Plant, ed., *Healing the Wounds: The Promise of Ecofeminism.* Philadelphia: New Society Publishers, 1989, pp. 174–85.

———. *Truth or Dare: Encounters with Power, Authority, and Mystery.* San Francisco: Harper & Row, 1990.

Stowasser, Barbara Freyer. *Women in the Qur'an: Traditions and Interpretation.* New York: Oxford University Press, 1994.

Swearer, Donald K. *The Buddhist World of Southeast Asia.* Albany: State University of New York Press, 1995.

Swidler, Leonard. *Women in Judaism: The Status of Women in Formative Judaism.* Metuchen, N.J.: Scarecrow Press, 1976.

Tambiah, Stanley Jeyaraja. *Buddhism and the Spirit Cults of North-east Thailand.* Cambridge: Cambridge University Press, 1970.

Tapper, Nancy. "*Ziyaret*: Gender, Movement, and Exchange in a Turkish Community," in Dale F. Eickelman and James Piscatori, eds., *Muslim Travellers: Pilgrimage, Migration, and the Religious Imagination.* London: Routledge, 1990, pp. 236–55.

Thiébaux, Marcelle. *The Writings of Medieval Women.* Garland Library of Medieval Literature, vol. 14, series B, New York: Garland Publishing, 1987.

Thompson, Catherine. "Women, Fertility and the Worship of Gods in a Hindu Village," in Pat Holden, ed., *Women's Religious Experience.* London: Croom Helm, 1983, pp. 113–31.

Tress, Madeleine. "Halakha, Zionism, and Gender: The Case of Gush Emunim," in Valentine M. Moghadam, ed., *Identity Politics and Women: Cultural Reassertions and Feminisms in International Perspective.* Boulder, Colo.: Westview Press, 1994, pp. 307–28.

Tsomo, Karma Lekshe, ed. *Sakyadhita: Daughters of the Buddha.* Ithaca, N. Y.: Snow Lion Publications, 1988.

Wadley, Susan S. "Hindu Women's Family and Household Rites in a North Indian Village," in Nancy Falk and Rita Gross, *Unspoken Worlds: Women's Religious Lives in Non-Western Cultures,* 2nd ed. Belmont, Calif.: Wadsworth, 1989, pp. 72–81.

———, ed. *The Powers of Tamil Women.* Syracuse, N.Y.: Maxwell School of Citizenship and Public Affairs, 1980.

Wadud-Muhsin, Amina. *Qur'an and Woman.* Kuala Lumpur: Penerbit Fajar Bakti, 1992.

Wagner, Roy. "Taboo," in Mircea Eliade, ed., *The Encyclopedia of Religion*, vol. 14. New York: Macmillan, 1987, pp. 233–36.

Walker, Alice. "The Right to Life: What Can the White Man Say to the Black Woman?," in Charlotte Watson Sherman, ed., *Sisterfire: Black Womanist Fiction and Poetry*. New York: HarperPerennial, 1994, pp. 93–98.

Ward, Hannah. "The Lion in the Marble: Choosing Celibacy as a Nun," in Linda Hurcombe, ed., *Sex and God: Some Varieties of Women's Religious Experience*. New York: Routledge & Kegan Paul, 1987, pp. 72–86.

Weaver, Mary Jo. "Who Is the Goddess and Where Does She Get Us," *Journal of Feminist Studies in Religion*, vol. 5 (1989), pp. 49–64.

Williams, Dolores S. "The Color of Feminism: Or Speaking the Black Woman's Tongue," *The Journal of Religious Thought*, vol. 43 (1986), pp. 42–58.

———. *Sisters in the Wilderness: The Challenge of Womanist God-Talk*. Maryknoll, N.Y.: Orbis Books, 1993.

Wilson, Katharina M., ed. *Medieval Women Writers*. Athens: University of Georgia Press, 1984.

Wolff, Pierre. *Discernment: The Art of Choosing Well*. Ligouri, Mo.: Triumph Books, 1993.

Woodhead, Linda. "Spiritualising the Sacred: A Critique of Feminist Theology," *Modern Theology*, vol. 13 (1997), pp. 191–212.

Yocum, Glenn. "Burning 'Widows,' Sacred 'Prostitutes,' and 'Perfect Wives': Recent Studies of Hindu Women," *Religious Studies Review*, vol. 20 (1994), pp. 277–85.

Young, Katherine K. "Hinduism," in Arvind Sharma, ed., *Women in World Religions*. Albany: State University of New York Press, 1987, pp. 59–103.

———. "Goddesses, Feminists and Scholars," in Arvind Sharma and Katherine Young, eds., *The Annual Review of Women in World Religions*, vol. 1. Albany: State University of New York Press, 1991, pp. 105–79.

———. "Women in Hinduism," in Arvind Sharma, ed., *Today's Woman in World Religions*. Albany: State University of New York Press, 1994, pp. 77–136.

Young, Serenity. *An Anthology of Sacred Texts by and About Women*. New York: Crossroad, 1993.

Index

Women
  academic and non-academic
    views of, 148
  and the
    education/socialization of
    children, 114
  anti-academic sentiments, 148
  as cause of religious schism, 34
  as irrational, 94
  as marginal, 83
    in religious practices/texts,
    2–3, 76–83
  as misbegotten males, 54
  as responsible for men's sexual
    reactions, 91
  as subjects of study, 12–13
  as subjects who speak, 109–14
  biological and social life-stages
    of, 59
  different views about
    belief/praxis among,
    146–50
  greater moral responsibilty,
    91
  identity/"self" of, 53
  papal teaching about, 25–34
  philosophical differences
    among, 142–43
  political differences among,
    144–46
  powerful women as
    manipulative/threatening,
    95
  prone to possession, 58
  synthesis of social and religious
    views of, 81
  Western/non-Western, 144–46
Women's spiritual groups, 61
Women's bodies, See Women's
    sexuality
  as sacred space, 120
  lack of control over, 90
  language about, 83
  phases of fertility, 84
Women's
    conferences/gatherings,
    148

Women's experience, See
    Motherhood
  as essentially different, 4
  as historically and culturally
    specific, 6–7
  black women's experience, 10
  conflicting perspectives on, 7
  connection between the
    varieties of, 4
  cultural and temporal
    differences in, 4
  definitions of, 5–7
  essentialist concepts of, 6–7,
    37–38
  feminist, womanist, mujerista
    views of, 6
  international dimension and
    pluralism, 5
  of oppression, 9
  relative importance of, 3
Women's identity
  biological and social focus, 59
  in relation to marriage, 59
Women's movements
  and new religious/spiritual
    identities, 126
  Western white women's agenda
    in, 144
Women's ordination
  as cause of schism, 45
  in Buddhism, 45, 143
  in the Anglican church, 45
  in the Catholic church, 26, 29,
    45
  in the Presbyterian Church of
    Australia, 77
Women's religious experience,
    See Women's sexuality
  and life-stages, 129
  and male religious
    professionals/male
    scholars, 2, 12, 27, 69
  as marginal, dangerous,
    superstitious, 71–74, 123
  in a variety of sociocultural
    groups, 41–48
  in the Catholic church, 28